GILA DESCENDING

~ ~ ~ ~ ~ ~ ~ ~ ~ ~ ~

A Southwestern Journey

by

M.H. Salmon

Illustrations by

Fred Barraza

High-Lonesome Books
Silver City, NM   88062

ACKNOWLEDGEMENTS

Thanks to George Valencia, Thayne Peters, Dusty Hunt, Randy Reiss and Charles Dixon for shuttle service; to the Gila National Forest and New Mexico Department of Game & Fish for information about the river, the region and the wildlife; to Fred Barraza for his talented artwork; and to Rojo and that Damn Cat for staying aboard even when my humor wasn't so good.

ISBN-13: 978-0944383-20-9
ISBN-10: 0-944383-20-3
Library of Congress Catalog Card # 87-82500

Fourth Edition
2006

AUTHOR'S NOTE

All that follows is based on fact. For rhetorical purposes I have re-ordered certain events. For a variety of reasons, certain characters depicted emerge in composite form. There is also a measure of opinion herein and of course you don't have to swallow any of that if you don't want to. But it all happened.

"But there hovers over many of the pages a shadowy ulterior purpose of pointing out to a bedeviled humanity that in the world of roots and clouds and wings and leaves there exists no Depression; that in its beauties and simplicities rather than from divers, bewildered senates and parliaments is man's peace most likely to be derived; that as life progressively adapts itself to its background of sun and soil, it gains in wholesomeness and sincerity."

Ross Calvin
Sky Determines

"The Colorado, entirely west of the Great Divide, might be called the river of the West; and the Rio Grande, entirely east of the divide, might be designated the international river. But the Gila is literally the river of the American Southwest. There is no other stream that even resembles it."

Edwin Corle

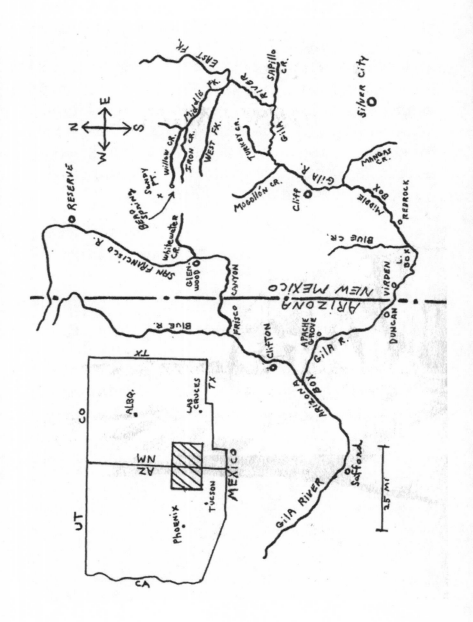

Also by M. H. Salmon

~~~

Non-fiction
Gazehounds & Coursing
Tales of the Chase
Catfish as Metaphor
Country Sports

Fiction
Home is the River
Signal to Depart

DEDICATION

For my mother,
and the memory of my father

Introduction to the Fourth Edition

In the spring of 1983 I made a three-week trip down the Gila River. Starting at the source waters of Bead Spring, Gila Wilderness, New Mexico, I hiked the first fifty to sixty miles to The Forks whence I canoed the rest of the way, well into Arizona. My hound-dog, Rojo, was there for the entirety while the unlikely tomcat was limited to the canoeing portion of the trip. We ended up taking out at the large diversion dam near Solomonville, Arizona, just upstream from the boomtown of Safford (talk about growth!), about a 220-mile journey in all.

The trip was variously a lark, a hoped-for personal restoration, and a chance to see the river in its (mostly) natural state before they dammed it up. I wrote a book about it all— *Gila Descending*—and it has been through several modest printings. The story of the trip can't change much—a small tale of personal history—but the story of the river ebbs and flows and continues to make the news. An update is in order.

At the time of the trip several water development interests were pushing a big Federal water project on the Gila, designed to remove 18,000 acre feet (af) (about 20%) from it's yearly flow. Namely, and mainly, these interests were: local boosters in the Silver City area, the Bureau of Reclamation, the New Mexico Interstate Stream Commission (ISC), and the State Engineer, the legendary, powerful, and extremely competent, Steve Reynolds. The project had been "authorized" by Congress in 1968 as part of the Central Arizona Project; in a deal to get New Mexico's support for the CAP Reynolds had "extorted" (his term) the "New Mexico unit" on the Gila. In 1983 it looked like it was just a matter of time until New Mexico's last free-flowing river got a big dam, its water destined for the only urban area in the region, Silver City, some 10,000 people living over the Continental Divide some 30 miles away. Thus my yen to make the trip before the natural river was gone.

New Mexico had a fabulous snowpack and run-off in the spring of '83; I got lucky and made my run. Better yet, though unrelated, troubles began to entangle the dam builders.

The Hooker Dam site, between Turkey Creek and Mogollón Creek, fell out as the preferred alternative because it would have pushed a lake twenty miles back up into the Gila Wilderness. In a new era of environmental awareness, this could not be done, even by Steve Reynolds. The Conner Dam site, 20 miles downstream in the Middle Box Canyon, became the preferred alternative of the boosters. It looked strong for a time in the mid-80s. Little by little, however, New Mexico's last unregulated flow was becoming a "cause" within the State's environmental community; at a public hearing in Silver City the conservationists outnumbered the boosters and Federal enthusiasm for the Conner proposal began to wane. The U.S. Fish & Wildlife Service and New Mexico Department of Game & Fish were even less cooperative. They opined that the riparian habitats to be drowned out by the dam were of the highest category and "could not be mitigated." And they documented two rare local minnows in that river reach, the spike dace and loach minnow, proposed them as "threatened" under the Endangered Species Act, and they were soon protected by Federal law. By the late 80s the idea of a mainstem dam on the Gila was abandoned by the Feds. Subsequently, a brief look at a diversion system with offstream storage in Mangas Creek was considered. It did not get far. It *might* have dodged the ESA problem but public opposition was still strong, the cost/benefit analysis, fairly done by the BOR, was negative, *very significant* aquifer storage in the Silver City area was made public (making new water from the distant Gila seem extravagant and superfluous), and there was the matter of the locals having to contract to pay their share of the total costs, which exceeded 100 million dollars. When the mayor of Silver City, himself an engineer, got a look at the cost of the water per acre foot he wisely declined the contract. Certain people can't see any rationale in a stream flow beyond diversion and consumption. Instream flows, which benefit fish, wildlife and recreation values, are not a "beneficial use," according to the old paradigm of Western water management. Yet in the space of a decade, what had looked like the last best hope of the boosters, developers, ISC and State Engineer, to dam the State's last river, had crumbled. As one of the BOR engineers told me over a beer: "In truth, this project was a dog from the start."

Well, the "dog" is back. In December 2004 President Bush signed the Arizona Water Settlements Act which settled Indian water rights claims in Arizona. Just as Steve Reynolds extorted a New Mexico unit in 1968 as a condition of New Mexico's support for the CAP, New Mexico's congressional delegation now got Arizona to OK another version of the Gila unit as payback for support of Arizona's new deal with the Indians. The settlement itself is enormous, involving over 2 billion dollars, and has been described as "pork wrapped in an Indian blanket." But, thanks to the US Congress and you the taxpayer, everybody got something, including New Mexico, which can count on $66 million for the four counties of Catron, Grant, Luna and Hidalgo "for any water related purpose," and another $62 million "if a Gila project is built."

To date, no project has been *officially* identified by the ISC. A mainstem dam is out; diversion to offstream storage in a side canyon is anticipated. *Unofficially*, both the ISC and the State Engineer have spoken of a massive pumping station, and infiltration gallery, between Turkey Creek and Mogollon Creek, a huge pipeline (since water could only be taken during short periods of high flows) to gravity feed downstream to a storage reservoir at Mangas Creek. The project has legs because in this case up to $128 million has already been approved by Congress.

But it's still a dog. In Congressional testimony in September, '03, New Mexico State Engineer John D'Antonio estimated a construction cost of $220 million, though he acknowledged on the record that others have put the cost at $300 million or more. The spike dace and loach minnow are still listed species and still inhabit the contested river miles. Silver City and environs, a recent hydrological study has shown, sit virtually astride an aquifer storage of 15.2 *million* acre feet to a depth of 600 feet. The town currently uses about 2800 af per year. Even with growth there is enough aquifer storage to last beyond a thousand years. A study by EcoNorthwest Inc. in 2005 showed this Mimbres aquifer water could be developed for 10 to 16 times *less* money per acre foot than that available under the State Engineer/ISC proposal for Gila River water. Why spend ten times more for water 30 miles away that's not needed in the first place? The resolution is obvious enough.

New Mexico should take the $66 million and divide it equally among the four counties (at about $16.5 million each, wisely invested, each county could count on about $1million per year in perpetuity). Catron County wants to restore watersheds to create more water for its San Francisco River. Fine. Grant County, where Silver City resides, would have funding to acquire additional water rights and drill new wells as needed. Luna and Hidalgo Counties use most of their water for irrigation agriculture. They would have the funding to convert to drip irrigation, a 40% to 50% savings per acre that would save far more water yearly than the ISC's proposed Gila project would supply. This political water fight is in full swing at this writing. Studies are underway but the ISC has made it clear that, regardless of the numbers or common sense, it is "going for the water." The next few years will tell the tale.

Meanwhile, the trip I took with Rojo and that damn cat is still available to you. In the spring of '05 my son Bud, age 10, and I made the "wilderness run" from Grapevine Campground to Mogollón Creek. New grazing restrictions have restored the riparian zone, narrowed and improved the river. And that includes the Middle Box, Lower Box, and the National Conservation Area where the Gila meets the Frisco in Arizona. ATV use is likewise eliminated in many areas along the river or at least better managed. Gila trout recovery has made progress and a downsizing to "threatened" is expected soon. This would allow for some catch and release fishing for the Gila's own unique strain of trout. Elsewhere in the cooler waters, browns, rainbows, and rainbow/Gila hybrids can still be had, and in the warmer waters, smallmouth bass, channel catfish, and flathead catfish and carp as long as your leg, await the angler. Flood, drought, and ash flows take their toll, but with improvements to the river, and sensible regulations, the fishing can only get better over time. Since 1983 I've become as much a fly fisher as a bait fisher; either way I'm not the best but it says something for the river that I've been doing pretty good. In sum, we have been gifted a wild river with a self-sustaining sport fishery, a number of rare endemic species, and perhaps the best birding in the Southwest! It should be an easy call but, like I said, powerful forces are going for the water, and they don't intend it for fish or birds.

More than 20 years ago, Rojo, the tomcat, and I saw the whole 220 miles of river in one trip. I thought at the time: *All said, there's not a better place anywhere in the West.* In spite of boosters, boomers, politicians, and certain government agencies, that's still true today. The Gila River is the last flow in New Mexico that can teach us what a natural river should be. Improbably, it still flows free. Enjoy it. Don't let them take it away.

M.H. Salmon
June, 2006

Note: For more information on the Gila River issues:
www.gilaconservation.org

PROLOGUE

Any journey taken on as pleasure or diversion will begin with the idea - something you conjure up and savor as fantasy - and only if there is sufficient inspiration therein does travel ever come to form and reality. It's not as if you're going to lose your job if you don't make the trip.

There is often as well the spur of discontent: a journey, more than a mere outing, involves a breaking away - a change of life for a time - and if everything is quite all right around home, you're likely not to go.

It is an unusual life that cannot find some discontent worth fleeing any week of the year. As for fantasy, I've spent far too much of my life with my mind off the present, off instead to someplace I've never been, to something I've never done. Being fond of map gazing, I had looked at the forest green of the great Gila Country on paper lots of times...and my mind would wander. Running my finger over the enticing names I have imagined exhaustive chases after bear in the Black Range; Smallmouth Bass, slick, vigorous, from the Gila's East Fork; and expeditions into the Burro Mountains where roams the occasional Coatimundi. Just to see one would be quite enough.

My scope over paper was never broad enough to conjure up the length of the Gila River. But out on a hunt one day, horseback with hounds over the Sacaton Mesa, the blue/black Mogollón Range (the source) was all day in distant view; overbearing, pervasive and snow-capped. By the time we'd reined around toward evening - headed for the barn and thoroughly outrun - I had gotten it into my mind to travel the Gila, from its beginnings on down to where it ceases to flow as a natural river. Fantasy and a modicum of discontent did the rest.

"I suppose some will wish to debate whether it is important to keep the primitive arts alive. I shall not debate it. Either you know it in your bones or you are very, very old."
        ~ Aldo Leopold

PART I   SIERRA DEL GILA

They call it the Gila (pronounced Heé-la) River by a long and convoluted explanation (each writer and historian has a version) whereby an unpronounceable Apache name was supposedly shortened and corrupted by the early Spanish explorers.   The explanation doesn't bear repeating here precisely because it would be long and convoluted.   Also possibly inaccurate. The best guess is that the word "Gila", like the word "Pecos" in eastern New Mexico and West Texas, doesn't really mean anything. Nonetheless one must approve of the appellation. The Apaches were the first people to really own this part of the world - nobody's ever owned it in quite such a way - and to work their name for all this into the musical Spanish language is appropriate. Couldn't be nicer really.

"Sierra del Gila" is a misnomer of sorts too. You won't find it on the maps; there is no "Gila Range" per se. The Middle and West Forks of the Gila River derive from high mountain springs in the Mogollón Mountains; they join in time and shortly the East Fork comes in from the Black Range. Once all three have gotten together you have the Gila River. The Black Range, the Mogollones, the Blue Range in nearby Arizona and other adjacent mountain groupings of the Gila drainage form, in my book, the Sierra del Gila. Again one must approve and thank the Spanish; the name is at once muscular and musical; it bespeaks both a rugged range and a fragile beauty.

~ ~ ~ ~ ~ ~

By late in the spring winter's snow is melting rapidly in the high country of the Sierra del Gila. Reports coming in to Gila Forest Headquarters indicated there were still significant drifts on the north slopes above 10,000 feet, but it sounded like I could get around all right up there and see and do what I had in mind without resorting to snowshoes or rescue by mule. I had assembled some backpacking gear for hiking the upper portion of the Gila, had a small canoe mostly ready for when I got to the East Fork confluence, and with things at home about as ordered and arranged for my absence as they were ever going to get, I could think of no good reason for hanging around any longer. I could think of several good reasons for getting the hell out.

Across the road a friend and neighbor, George Valencia, had just gotten out of school for the summer - he's about 17 years old. He would be looking after some half dozen hounds while I was gone and, approached that morning, he liked the idea of driving me out and dropping me off way up high. I tossed the pack sack and a hound dog in the back of the truck and took one last look around deciding, inevitably, that whatever it was I was leaving behind that I'd wish I had when I got up into the high-lonesome, I'd find out about soon enough.

The Mimbres River Valley where I live was deceptively green as we left. Once away from there crossing over the first hills at Santa Rita the usual parched brown of a southwestern spring was obvious. But disconcerting. Other places I've lived - Texas, Minnesota, New York - it rains in the spring. I've lived in New Mexico long enough to know it doesn't rain in the spring here, at least not very much or often, but not long enough that it doesn't still strike me as odd.

At my suggestion we stopped in Silver City for a feed. I thrive on juxtapositions, contrasts. About the tackiest thing you can do before heading out alone into the last great wilderness in the Southwest is to stop at a fast food place, stand in line with the hordes and order up about as much as you figure you can possibly stand; this would be the last meal of its kind for some time. A *McDonald's* will of course serve you all you can pay for. I paid for it all - me and George both - we ate it all (My God!) and were off again, heading north up Highway 180.

Crossing the Gila, the lower Gila, at Cliff, I noted there was plenty of water; enough to float a canoe certainly. This was reassuring for I hoped to have my canoe on that river in a week or so...if all went well.

On up the road the first of several pretty girls, each with a blaze orange vest and a flag, brought us to a series of temporary halts for road repairs. Used to be they'd give that flag job to the biggest, burliest guy on the crew but not any more. Now they give the job to a girl and I don't know if it's simply the improvement of not having to look at one of those potbellied men, but it seems to me they're most all good looking. These sure were. I obeyed their commands, didn't say

3

much, and watched appreciatively while considering something else there wouldn't be any of for the next few weeks. George meanwhile was not without comment. He's one of those guys; has this smile at once ingenuous and disarming and always with something to say when there's a girl around. What he said to these girls would have bordered on rude coming from me but he's got that smile. At each stop he was killing them in two languages.

All this of course is only fair. For years men corralled all the road jobs while women, driving slowly through the crew, checked them out. Now, in fairness, some of these jobs go to women, and we men get to return the compliment.

We got the go-ahead from the last pretty girl and drove on, turning off near Glenwood to start up that tortuous little road to the ghost town of Mogollón (say Mō-gō-yōn). Mogollón is in Catron County, which at nearly 7,000 square miles is easily larger than the state of Connecticut, yet is inhabited by less than 3,000 people, a combination that leaves the county with numerous quality of life characteristics found almost nowhere else in America. They named the town of Mogollón and the Mogollón Range and Mogollón Creek after an early Spanish governor (back when New Mexico was territory of Spain). I probably shouldn't say this because Mogollón is one of many things in the region I wouldn't want to spoil, but this place is everything a ghost town nestled at 7,000 feet in the mountains ought to be. It's the last word in dilapidated quaint, there's a creek running through, and though there has been some refurbishing done here and there by the town's sparse residents, Mogollón hasn't really been discovered yet. Butch Cassidy hung around here, and Ben Lilly and Victorio and other notables. Driving up the little narrow street you get out, if

4

you're any kind of a photographer, put on a wide-angle lens and take a picture. It's the obvious thing to do. Itchy to get into the wilderness I took no pictures and did not stop.

The blacktop road, such as it is, soon ends, but we continued on, up, up and up. Officially, this is a state highway, #78, and it's on the map. In fact it's a little bitty, maybeso kind of dirt road. For about five months each year it's shut down by snow; the highway department doesn't even try. A few years back a friend of mine I won't name was part of a crew instructed to assess the cost and value of turning #78 into an all-weather, all season highway. Being a wilderness lover of intelligence and tact he did not hesitate in his report to emphasize the great cost of paving this stretch, fencing off the livestock, and the effects of such a project on the last great wilderness in the Southwest. He did his job well and with any luck it will be a long time or hopefully forever before they think again to ruin State Road #78 with pavement or progress.

I pulled off by the Sandy Point Trailhead where my trip would really begin. We were maybe an hour out of Glenwood but now in a different world, having witnessed desert grassland yield to piñon/juniper, to Ponderosa Pine, and finally at 9,000 feet and nearly a mile above that town, fir, spruce, aspen. I detected a distinct scarcity of oxygen and something new: humidity. It's lush that high in the Mogollónes, by any standards. It rains there, even in the spring. Wandering around a bit I easily imagined springs and snow pack nearby that could be the beginnings of a river.

I handed George the keys and a ten spot. I told him not to spend it all in one place and to watch out he didn't get kidnapped by one of those flag girls on the way home. Then, tucking a big ol' ugly pinch of *Red Man* between cheek and gum, I

5

shouldered that backpack I knew already I was destined to dislike intensely, whistled for the dog and stepped into the Sierra
del Gila.

~ ~ ~ ~ ~ ~

The trail leading away from Sandy Point is called the
Crest Trail (by way of confusion so is another trail that takes
one along the Continental Divide not far to the east in the
Black Range) and you're not many steps off Highway #78 when
you are faced by a forest sign that says you are now entering
the Gila Wilderness. This is significant. It is an official Federal
Forest Service designation and indicates among other things:
no trail bikes, no snowmobiles, no pickup trucks, no chainsaws,
no *Dairy Queen*, TV or roads. They mean it too. A few years
back some off-road vehicle enthusiasts managed to get their
four-wheel drive pickup back into the wilderness a ways and got
caught. They had to walk out and were heavily fined. Com-
pounding their loss and elevating their humility, they had to
hire an outfitter with a team of mules to go back in there and
pull the machine out beyond the wilderness boundary before
they were allowed to even start the engine. Beyond the restrictions, what's left that you *are* allowed to do in a wilderness can
keep any *real* outdoor person happy. You can walk or ride a
horse or paddle a canoe. You can hunt, fish, trap, pick
blueberries, watch the birds, camp wherever you want and
there's no charge.

People in southwest New Mexico are justly proud of the
Gila country and are fond of telling people that the Gila Wilderness is both the first and largest wilderness area in the lower
48. It is the first, but it's not the largest; there are several in
Idaho and Montana that are larger. The Gila Wilderness covers
about 600,000 acres (the Gila National Forest, wilderness and

otherwise, nearly 3.5 million acres). Adjacent to it, separated narrowly by another of those maybeso kind of dirt roads (State "Highway" #61), is the Aldo Leopold Wilderness. The two used to be one. The Aldo Leopold Wilderness takes up a good chunk of the Black Range, over 200,000 acres. To the west, not far, is the Blue Range Primitive Area, much of which lops over into Arizona, another 200,000 acres. Into this one corner of the Southwest they have managed to save a million acres pretty much as nature intended. There will never be enough designated wilderness to suit me. At this writing, only about 2% of the State of New Mexico is protected as wilderness. Still, a million acres is not insignificant. Many wilderness designations are pockets of land less than 100,000 acres. A million acres is enough to support the *wild* in the larger word.

You hike the Crest Trail gaining elevation, some 1500 feet, before things begin to level off at Hummingbird Saddle. Climbing - with that egregious pack on my back - I was sweating like a horse. It was work and it was warm and there was that surprising humidity. But with a few rest stops along the way none of it was causing me to breathe all that hard and my legs felt good. I watched my companion carefully. Rojo is a hound of course and hounds hunt. Rojo hunts coyotes. He had his instructions and we'd been out before and he always seemed to sense the difference between a hunt and an outing. Still, I was talking to the boy every little bit and I whistled him up a couple of times; I didn't on this trip want him baying over the next mountain on a hot track. He was doing fine. He'd disappear up the trail for a while and then I'd see him standing there waiting, making sure I kept pace. Occasionally he'd meander off the trail and when he did that he'd invariably come back on to the trail behind me and run by, having fun. We'd get along. And there aren't many coyotes up that high anyway.

Bead Spring. This is the start of Willow Creek which flows and sparkles on down to where it joins Gilita Creek and forms the Middle Fork of the Gila River. Put to naming just one place, I suppose you'd have to call Bead Spring the "source" of the Gila River. There are others, of course. Gilita Creek comes down off Bearwallow Mountain but at a lesser altitude. Cub Creek, White Creek - these are high, chill emanations of the West Fork. Iron Creek off Whitewater Baldy probably starts from higher up but its beginnings are less precise. Bead Spring wells up out of the ground not as a trickle but as a stream in progress. A lovelier place is hard to imagine. Englemann Spruce, Blue Spruce and aspen all around, I dug into my pack, found my tin cup and quaffed an elixir that will make your teeth ache in mid-July. I looked for beads. Forty years ago, they tell me, you could easily find and walk off with one hundred. I found one and put it back.

Options. Options force decisions. Decisions are one of the many things you go to the wilderness to escape but, really, there are always options and decisions to be made. Considering Bead Spring, I also considered that the logical thing, it being the source, would be to follow Willow Creek on down to the Middle Fork. But I hadn't seen any snow yet and I wanted to, to complete the juxtaposition with the desert-lands of central Arizona a few weeks hence. Also, Willow Creek soon leaves the wilderness and streams through Willow Creek campground, Gilita campground, and runs parallel for a ways with State Highway #78. There'd be people and cars and picnic tables and beer cans and such. The option was to continue on up the Crest Trail to Hummingbird Saddle, camp near Hummingbird Spring, cross snow on the north side of Whitewater Baldy, then start down, finally, towards Iron Creek, coming out on the Middle Fork a few miles below Snow Lake. Wilderness all the way. I had a few hours of light left and Rojo, after splashing around a little, was already nosing his way further up the Crest Trail. I followed the dog.

~ ~ ~ ~ ~ ~

It rained that night at Hummingbird Saddle and I found out that my $21 Government surplus tent leaked at the seams. Not surprising; indeed, when you pay $21 for a Government surplus tent and find nothing worse than a slight leak at the seams you can figure you've gotten off easy. I got off easy. By the time I realized my sleeping bag (also a cheapie) was wet it was good light, the rain had stopped, and Rojo and I crawled out to see the kind of sharp blue sky that often follows showers in the spring.

The high country of the Mogollón Mountains lies within the *Hudsonian* zone - that life zone that forms just below *Tundra/Alpine* - and anywhere you've got varieties of spruce plus aspen growing in large and lush profusion you can assume a lot of precipitation. Records of precipitation within the Gila Wilderness are hard to come by because nobody lives there; nobody's around each day to check the bottle. The Gila National Forest reports 40 inches a year as a fair average for any place approaching 10,000 feet in the Mogollónes. This includes rain and melted snow. Snowfall, before it settles and/or melts, is surely over 100 inches a year and may be twice that. The snow marker on Whitewater Baldy at 10,750 feet averages over 200 inches of snowfall per year, according to the U. S. Geological Survey. In the Mogollón Mountains the popular concept of New Mexico as a desert does not apply.

SIERRA DEL GILA

SIERRA DEL GILA

They claim the average rainfall in New Mexico is twelve inches per year. This is not very helpful as the convolutions of physiography statewide make the precipitation notably fractious. Probably no more than 20% of New Mexico gets enough rainfall - say twenty inches - to grow a pine tree. This means that mountain groupings like the Mogollónes, the Black Range, the Sacramentos or Sangre de Cristos are verdant islands in a sea of grassland and desert. Given that ten inches or less of rainfall per year qualifies as desert, great ecological extremes are found in New Mexico, especially southwest New Mexico. Starting at forty inches per year at Bead Spring you travel through five life zones on down to perhaps eight inches per year by the time you reach the Gila's juncture with the Arizona border, 150 miles by the current. Less as the crow flies. Up high it looks like Canada. Down below it's Chihuahuan Desert. All in the southwestern part of the state.

There is no *Alpine* zone in southwest New Mexico. None of the peaks top 11,000 feet although a number come close. There are higher mountains over by Ruidoso and up around Taos, and ski resorts there have given New Mexico a measure of fame as a winter wonderland. None of that applies in the Sierra del Gila. A few hardy souls trek the Crest Trail and others in the high country on snowshoes or cross-country skis, but the lack of access in winter limits the human incursion to those who really want to be there. Hummingbird Saddle is four life zones removed from desert. It is as well a measure of how important easy access is to modern outdoor recreation, for about mid-February it is as deserted, albeit beautiful, a place as you'll find in the Southwest.

The campground by Hummingbird Spring was not deserted in late spring when Rojo and I passed through. There

11

was a small community camped about, mostly a group of young people and the two or three counselors that had them fairly well in hand. There was also a man and woman accompanied by a couple of Pit Bulls. Rojo, really still a pup, wanted no part of them as we passed by the evening before; they had come out from behind their owners' tent thoroughly and typically pugnacious, but what the boy lacked in grit he made up for in speed. Rojo is not your ordinary hound. By breeding he is 1/2 Treeing Walker (a coonhound breed), 1/4 Bluetik (another coonhound) and 1/4 Staghound (rough-coated Greyhound). The latter, his grandmother, bequeathed him his long red coat, bearded face, and an incredibly smooth, swift, ground-eating stride. If those two Pit Bulls made him look cowardly as they chased him up the trail they were left for their part looking foolish trying to keep up in tight, over-muscled pursuit.

I was inclined to spend some time at Hummingbird Saddle (this would quite literally be the high point of the trip) but then I never expected the crowds. I had found a little flat place off in the trees the night before to place my camp - I could take a leak or talk to the dog without drawing peculiar glances from the troops - but this was not the way they describe wilderness in the brochures. As I had done the night before I built a small, quick fire and prepared my freeze-dried gruel - got my breakfast over with. The cup of coffee that followed I savored. And I thought it over.

I decided to break camp. With an early start I could easily reach Iron Creek for second camp and there perhaps focus upon the sharp solitude one can rightfully expect from a wilderness venture.

My sack was soon packed and I rolled up the bag and the tent and mounted both on the frame. I leaned it all against a tree and followed by the dog took my canteen down the little trail to Hummingbird Spring. It hadn't the flow of Bead Spring but the water was just as good and even without any Hummingbirds around it was a lovely setting with a grand overview to the south and west. Hummingbird Spring, I decided, is *the* highest source of Gila River water; the flow does eventually end up there, on over in Arizona, via Whitewater Creek and the San Francisco River. This struck me at the time as an interesting thought and curious connection, but the Frisco would be another river trip. I filled the canteen, started back up the trail and promptly met a young woman.

I had noticed her the evening before. Rojo, ambassador-at-large, had wandered over by a campfire surrounded by teens and counselors and made his usual greeting. He was well received. This girl, especially, seemed to like dogs and smiled my way. I was not unfriendly but in the near dark I wasn't sure if I was waving at an adult or a teeny-bopper and presently I called Rojo back lest he get into the hotdogs. The next morning by Hummingbird Spring I could see that she was old enough.

This was a large, healthy looking sort of young woman. Robust I'd even say. And buxom, as they used to say. Handsome rather than pretty. Attractive certainly. She hit me right away with several questions regarding plants and trees this high up. I meandered around the subject a while but what little I provided was necessarily vague and I don't think any news to her. The conversation flowed on easily from there nonetheless. We discussed the up and coming attempts by the enemy to dam the Gila River in New Mexico and struck a mutually sympathetic chord. Empathizing, she hoped her charges were not overly disturbing. Other things were discussed. We'd been at it quite a while before the conversation revealed we were each

13

breaking camp and headed in opposite directions. We parted with a promise to write which neither one of us kept. The moment had passed.

Once more burdened over the shoulders and back I left Hummingbird Saddle pondering my fate (or fortune) just transpired...

...Lost in love - more than once - with an utterly feckless personality, my response to what I could no longer have was invariably to have all I could. Over the course of a year, if you've got the temerity to tote it all up, an alarming figure accrues: a myriad of relationships, largely tactile in nature, eagerly sought and ultimately desultory; frantically engaging venereal release in an attempt to erase an evil memory, I merely succeeded in smearing it around. I've never been there but on the couch I believe it's referred to as "compulsive behavior." Could be. Certainly, towards the last, there was no one more feckless than I.

I wasn't traveling the Gila River in search of any more of that.

Nice girl though; we might could get along. The novelist Doris Lessing (back when she was still making sense) had a phrase: "unfulfilled possibilities." Ah Well!

~ ~ ~ ~ ~ ~

Where the snow was gone a variety of grasses had come in and the trees and shrubs already leafing out with tiny mountain flowers providing specks of color here and there, but in the first large shady spot the drift was several feet deep over the trail. It had settled with melt and had been trod upon so it was an easy thing to walk on top till the next patch of sun revealed the trail once again. Pausing to look on up the north slope towards the top of Whitewater Baldy I could see acres of white that would be there for weeks to come. This was the stuff that provided the runoff and recharged the aquifers that everyone from canoeists putting in at the East Fork to farmers in central Arizona relied upon for sustenance, commerce, and pleasures of a free-flowing stream. It was my pleasure to spend some time in late spring walking on the white stuff while crossing north facing slopes within the Gila Wilderness. And Rojo got down on his back several times and had a good roll in the snow.

In places - like where we turned off to head down the Iron Creek Trail - the aspen groves were pure, with spruce all around but none within. Where the big spruce stands were awesome these aspen groupings were pretty. Not as pretty I suppose had these aspens had white skins. These were mostly green-skinned aspens. I'm not botanist enough to know (I make no claims to botany at all) if it's the soil or if this is a sub-species (I've read that it's age yet I've seen big, old aspens that were still white), but I do know that in the Southwest white-skinned aspens impress tourists, photographers and writers with poetic aspirations, while the green-skinned variety remains largely unattended. I don't believe, for example, that I've ever seen photographs of green-skinned aspens in the *Arizona Highways* magazine. These would be sent back with a rejection slip.

Aspens are nice trees, but white or green they really can't compare with the White Paper Birch if you've lived in places like northern Minnesota or the Adirondaks of New York state. In northern Minnesota the aspen is ubiquitous and has earned the uninspiring nickname "popple." It is known there primarily as a tree that burns rapidly and with little heat in the wood stove, leaving a lot of creosote in the chimney with which you may one day set your house on fire. The skin of the White Paper Birch can form a canoe if you've got the talent. Its leaves in the fall are even more various and brilliantly hued

than those of the aspen and the chunks burn and heat in the wood stove like hard coal. I was never much impressed by aspens when I lived in northern Minnesota but I must admit they're looking better all the time in New Mexico. Surround your aspens with desert and you've got quite a tree!

The Iron Creek Trail brought me gradually but steadily into a lower altitude. Initially it doesn't run along Iron Creek at all but parallel to it and high above. This irritated me because I wanted to be traveling as much as possible along water sources of the Gila River, but it looked to be quite a jungle in the canyon below so I stayed on the trail and trod along without resting, thinking I'd make seven miles to Iron Creek Pond before setting my pack down. The aspens stayed with me for most of that stretch. Gradually, however, the spruce gave way to Douglas Fir and I realized I was passing through the *Canadian* life zone. The country began to open up a little. Where it did there was some knee-high, green grass with fir, aspen and soon some Ponderosa Pine scattered about. It was easy to see how long ago they came to call these open areas "parks." On the edge of one of these parks three cow elk came up from out of nowhere and ran across at an angle, headed for the heavy timber. I hollered at the hound but he bounded over there and intercepted the last elk just before she hit the trees. She wheeled about on the rearhand like a frightened horse before disappearing into the woods and for just that fraction it looked like he was right underneath her. He came running back to me like he was still chasing something. In fear now of both elk and a whipping he began to wiggle all around with his tail between his legs and his lips pulled back over his teeth in a most submissive grin. I said, "Wipe that smile off your face!" We would have no more of elk chasing.

17

Arriving at Iron Creek Pond in a slight rain; the water in this *cienega* of maybe five acres was murky but I liked the way the Ponderosa stood tall and in scattered patterns, rimmed around the edges. I hadn't had my pack off my back in a number of hours as the calves of my legs and that place where my shoulders met my neck were well aware. Each and every backpacker knows the symptoms. I needed a drink from the canteen and some dried fruit. I set the pack down.

Despite an affinity for and experience in lengthy trips into wild country, I had resisted the social phenomenon of backpacking for many years. Upon reflection I'm not wild about the sport, although even for me it has its place and its advantages. Down below, within the Gila Middle Box Canyon, I like to pack in on foot - a hike of several hours - set up a catfish camp for a stay of one or two nights, then pack out. No use getting all geared up with a horse or mule for a minor jaunt like that. On an extended trip of fifty miles plus, such as from Sandy Point to the East Fork, I would much prefer to have a large animal to ride and another to do the work. A horse or mule or even a burro could carry three or four times my load with half the effort, providing creature comforts and more savory rations and someone besides Rojo to talk to and scratch behind the ears when my humor is good. Some unexpected moving around and that ever-present condition of penury had caused me to unload the two horses I once had, leaving me a-foot in the Sierra del Gila.

Basically, I see backpacking as geared more to those who like to wear short pants (I have always felt foolish in short pants) and who don't mind bright colors like blaze orange or brilliant yellow (an abomination in a wilderness) or the eating of freeze dried food (ish!). I am reminded at times of Ben Lilly, the

SIERRA DEL GILA

legendary bear and lion hunter of this same Gila country and a hero of sorts of mine, who did most of his hunting on foot. True. But even ol' Ben afoot often made use of a pack animal, providing food and rudimentary camp facilities for himself and five or six hounds on excursions of two to three weeks at a time. This is a fair compromise and still not a bad way to travel in the back country of the Southwest. And I have a picture of Ben Lilly. He's riding a stubby burro and he's geared up for long range. On overnight hunts with the hounds I've done the same sort of thing, with a small pack on my back, a bedroll behind the saddle and a sack of stuff hanging off each side of the saddle horn. Call it go-light horse packing. Or equine backpacking. It only requires one animal and is also a fair compromise in wilderness travel. It will get further and serious consideration from me before I once again set out on a fifty to sixty mile wilderness trip on foot.

Doubtless my thoughts on backpacking show a subjective prejudice, reflecting the fact that, aesthetically, I like the sight and company of a horse, mule or burro in the Sierra del Gila. Equine history and tradition is strong here, be the riders Apache, Spanish or Anglo. But I am perhaps not the best one to talk about it. What I know about horses and mules you could put in your shirt pocket and still not know it was there. And besides, there I was at Iron Creek Pond seated underneath a Ponderosa, leaning back against my forest green backpack and rolled-up orange tent, eating dehydrated apricots. And very much enjoying myself.

Loaded up again, I circled Iron Creek Pond and peered at the mud flats to see who'd been there before me. Raccoon had been there, and deer and elk and a Great Blue Heron and a

Black Bear, whose print from a hind foot looked, as always, shockingly human.

It was not a long walk from the pond on a sharply down-hill trail to Iron Creek. I was pleased to get there. With the exception of one short detour, I'd now be following the currents from here on down into central Arizona...or for however far I got. Also, it looked like it might rain harder at any time and I wanted to make camp.

Moving downstream a ways I found nobody and set up a camp right on the creek rather to my liking. I propped my tent up straightaway and put everything inside in case the weather got worse, then, feeling a nap coming on, the hound and I crawled inside. Muscles were still sore and knotted, but I knew the cure for both was the same - flake out.

I don't know how much later it was when I woke up but by the light left in the sky I guessed it was early evening. It was still clouded over but the drizzle had stopped and indeed had never really amounted to much. Muscle discomfort was largely gone. As exercise, my first extended backpacking trip wasn't going to jerk me down too bad.

Not that I was in shape for it. People who are flat-bellied and flat-assed like me - "scrawny" if you had to put it into a word - are often seen by those who aren't (i.e. potbellied and lard-assed) as being "in shape." Scrawniness is more often the result of a blessed metabolism. I avoid exercise for exercise sake, but simply as a matter of lifestyle am fairly active. But not in shape. I think even those who are in shape are only in shape for their particular activities. A guy I know can run marathons and jog on till time unknown but he told me that on his first backpacking expedition he felt muscles, (felt them unpleasantly) he didn't know he had. His heart and lungs were good but certain specifics had not been stressed. The hard core backpacker who suddenly spends eight hours on a horse will feel eighty years old when he eases himself into the hot tub later that night. Rojo, who was on the go, mostly at a run, while I was just plodding along - he was in shape. But then his duties in life are limited and not various, consisting primarily in running a coyote down and putting him on the ground. And keeping me company.

I got a fire going, a bigger and cheerier fire than the night before, and considered my culinary options. Had I been active along Iron Creek in the mist instead of asleep, I might have had trout for supper. Instead it was spaghetti. I got the water boiling, poured out the package and presto! A complete meal. I will say some good things for freeze-dried food. It fills you up and keeps you going; it does the job. It is also of course light and unobtrusive in the pack. It is all they say it is except savory; not awful, but it removes all the pleasant anticipation from eating, and the eating of good food is a particular pleasure in the outdoors. Freeze-dried food has never promoted the pleasurable sin of gluttony. I would have my treats however. A pipeful of tobacco, a custom blend from a drug store in Silver City. A cup of coffee, instant to be sure but made with good water and black as pitch; it would float a nail. And then...from the pack...I removed a pint of pleasure known as *Southern Comfort*. A double shot with a dollop of Iron Creek water as coolant and mixer in concert with the campfire and a sleeping hound augmented an ambience not unlike what is described in the wilderness brochures, or the outdoor magazines I occasionally write for.

Well past dark a couple of coyotes started yipping and not far away. This turned my head and caused Rojo to lift his

from his tight curl. I promptly mentioned his name in a certain tone before he could gather his thoughts or his legs underneath. We listened, a bit tense and not moving, till the primal communication of little wolves had passed. Speaking out, sounding off like that, they continue to stir coyote hunters and those who oppose coyote hunters and most anyone else in between who has heard them in a pensive moment. The spirit of the wilderness? Nowdays, I guess they are, along with the Black Bear who stood in the mud at Iron Creek Pond. But then the spirit of the wilderness, at least in the Gila, has been both tainted and withdrawn, not so much by the presence of brightly colored backpackers as by the absence of animals far more wild than the coyote and more awesome even than the Black Bear. And yet more fragile than either. I speak (and think) of the larger wolves, and the Grizzly Bear.

~ ~ ~ ~ ~ ~

You walk into the Villagrá Building in Santa Fé which houses the New Mexico Department of Game & Fish and head up the stairs to the second floor two steps at a time. At the top, right there, is an impressive display: the well preserved hide and head mount of a Grizzly Bear. A placard gives some details. It is explained that this was one of New Mexico's final Grizzly Bears, taken in the northern part of the state circa 1923 (the very last, probably, was an even larger brute killed in the Black Range of the Gila Wilderness in 1931). The placard ends with the oft quoted plea from Aldo Leopold: "Relegating Grizzlies to Alaska is about like relegating happiness to heaven; one may never get there."

Question. Can one assume from this official display that the New Mexico Department of Game & Fish holds that the state would be richer environmentally with a population of

Grizzly Bears at loose in the wild? I haven't taken a poll. But in a variety of informal conversations, department personnel in high and low offices have expressed to me both regret at the loss of the Grizzly and *sympathy* for the *idea* of its reintroduction. I have found similar viewpoints in talking, again off the record, with Gila National Forest personnel. At this juncture the official display in the Villagrá Building remains - shall I say it - an empty gesture. There is no official movement afoot to bring the Grizzly back to New Mexico, or anywhere else in the Southwest. Still, one cannot discount the sympathy expressed. It's genuine and could one day produce action. But first...what happened?

It is generally stated that the Grizzly Bear, and the wolf, were extirpated from most of their original range because they were "in conflict with man." This is not precisely true. Even back in 1911 when Ben Lilly first set foot in New Mexico and promptly started on the track of a Grizzly in Hidalgo County, the bear was in conflict with very few men, almost all of them connected to the livestock industry. Ben got his bear and within twenty-five years he and a few others, as part of or at the behest of that industry, had gotten the rest. A more enlightened view of predators was still decades away.

The situation regarding the wolf - in southwest New Mexico the sub-species Mexican Wolf and Mogollón Wolf - is similar. The old Cloverdale wolf route, again in Hidalgo County below Lordsburg, was shut off during the 1940's; these were the last wolves in New Mexico, albeit, towards the last, these were wolves *of Mexico* who occasionally crossed the border *into New Mexico* on hunting trips. The decline and fall of Arizona's wolves followed a similar schedule. A few Mexican Wolves, perhaps fifty, remain in northern Chihuahua with a few others in captivity here in the states. A Mexican Wolf captive breeding program received a cover story in *New Mexico Wildlife* a couple of years ago. The author, at that time a part of the Department of Game & Fish, was involved in the program and made an elegant and well researched plea for the preservation of this animal. It was suggested (implied more than stated) that the animals would be better off preserving themselves in the wild. But of course! The preservation in a zoo of an animal symbolic of wilderness is surely a contradiction of terms. I'll concede it's better to keep them alive as captives than to lose the gene pool entirely. But in *New Mexico Wildlife*, despite tacit approval for the *idea* of reintroduction, the suggestion that some wolves be turned loose was couched in the most tentative terms. The issue was skirted. I saw a grim, tight-lipped stockman, tanned, squinty-eyed, his stetson pulled down low over the forehead, overlooking the author's typewriter.

There is an irony here that ought to be obvious. The Gila Wilderness was probably the last place where New Mexico's wolves and grizzlies denned up. It was established in 1924 to preserve the original character of a relatively pristine ecosystem. No one would argue that that original character included the region's original inhabitants, its native or indigenous species. Yet two of the Gila's indigenous species, and the two most magnificent at that, were eliminated to protect an imported, non-indigenous, domesticated animal, the common cow, a handful of which roamed the Gila Wilderness in 1924. It is due to the ongoing presence of a relative handful of these non-native bovines that the Gila National Forest and the New Mexico Department of Game & Fish continue to wince when the subject of wolf or Grizzly re-introduction comes up.

SIERRA DEL GILA

The "value" of preserving native wilderness creatures like wolves and Grizzly Bears - indeed the value of preserving wilderness at all - is essentially a metaphysical question. An individual's response to the question depends I suspect on one's sense of aesthetics, or lack thereof, regarding wildlife and the great outdoors. This is the main reason defending such as wild wolves, grizzly bears, and wilderness is so difficult - you can't make the defense on economic grounds. Any defense, or promotion, is essentially philosophical, any articulation is in aesthetic terms. True enough, at times those of use who are wont to defend such as wilderness or wildlife will come across with arguments that relate to tourism and the recreation business, in hopes of assuaging the opposition. These arguments are often weak and, at least in my case, always hypocritical. We're not defending dollars and cents, jobs, growth or livelihood; we're defending amenities. It's a tough defense, what with "progress" in our time defined not in terms of how well we save wild rivers, endangered species, open space, historic structures, or archaic pursuits, but rather with regards to how well we continue to pour on the coals. The worth, the value, of amenities is hard to articulate. Such thoughts go over the heads of many and meet a brick wall with others. Either that or we haven't learned the proper articulation. This has never been more true than in our so far futile attempts to restore the wolf and what the old timers called "big bears" to the wild in the great Southwest. Even the best of us has failed.

In his *Sand County Almanac* Aldo Leopold, a professional forester, considers the metaphysical question and, as only an artist can do, develops an aesthetic into a cogent rationale for the preservation of wild country and its native creatures. It is wonderful reading and has had significant influence on the public at-large as well as professionals in fields like forestry and wildlife management. It has not, it seems, had much influence on people who raise cattle and sheep. A different rationale is needed for that.

Any proposal for the revival of wolves or grizzlies in the Southwest ought to require that the proponents climb over the fence into the stockman's pasture and take a look at some of the carcasses. Predatory animals - coyotes, Black Bears, Mountain Lions, Grizzly Bears, wolves, eagles - kill domestic livestock. The coyotes and eagles are particularly hard on sheep. Trendy animal rights types and other birds of paradise tend to think not, though even they will admit (the thought no doubt pains them) that these two catch lots of jackrabbits, an elusive creature if there ever was one. A newborn lamb is about the size of an adult Blacktail Jackrabbit, seven to eight pounds, and a lot more vulnerable. Numbers of them each year are lost to coyotes and eagles. Wolves kill moose where moose are the available quarry. If they can do it to moose they can do it to a steer. A female lion in the lower Gila country earned for herself a measure of fame. She wore a collar and transmitter and was followed by wildlife biologists. Her specialty was elk. She'd sprint, leap and latch onto the neck, taking the animal's snout head-on between impressive jaws. After several minutes of the most astounding thrashing about, the elk would die of suffocation. She did it time and again. She weighed eighty-eight pounds. Could she do as well with a horse or heifer? Would she refrain because the animal was domesticated and belonged to someone? Finally, the bears. They are omnivorous, not consistent predators. Still, by their very power, they can and do kill when the need or urge is upon them.

SIERRA DEL GILA

To try to deny that predators kill domestic livestock or to maintain that the kill is insignificant (when you're in business for yourself and on the fringe of profit and loss, any kill is significant) is ignorance and head-in-the-sand folly. Nonetheless stockmen, for the most part, don't hate predatory animals (though they often tote around some inflated fears of them); they simply hate losing money to the critters. It's a dollars and cents issue to the stockman and thus a rationale derived from an aesthetic holds little bite.

In southeast New Mexico a lot of sheep are raised and a lot of government (public) money is spent to keep the coyote population in that area sparse and thereby reduce the sheep kill. Government trappers are employed, aerial gunning is used, and depending on the administration in Washington, poison bait stations may be set out (the presence of poison and cyanide "coyote getters" in southern New Mexico has effectively placed large areas of public land off limits to a variety of public recreation). The coyote is not a threatened species, not even in southeast New Mexico where the pressure is severe; short of poison and cyanide guns and their unintended effects, I don't see anything wrong with the sheep rancher killing all the coyotes he feels it necessary to kill, but whether he should get public money to do it is highly debatable. They might as well give it to the corn farmer when the army worms erupt. Or to the ski resort owner when it fails to snow. Hell, give it to me! I got caught in a flash flood last year, totaled my pickup and like to killed myself. Struck down by the vicissitudes of nature.

The coyote in New Mexico is not protected at any time of the year; the rancher is not restricted in protecting his stock from coyotes. An interesting juxtaposition can be had by also considering the situation of an endangered species, a protected predator, like the wolf in northern Minnesota.

There is a lot of defacto wilderness in northern Minnesota. Even prior to federal wolf protection in the 1970's there were 1200 to 1500 Timber Wolves roaming around up there. While I was roaming around up there I saw three of these wolves at loose in the wild and in that consider myself luckier than most of you. Since the Timber Wolf became an endangered species in the early 1970's, the population of the animal in Minnesota has stabilized at perhaps two thousand. The range of the animal has increased somewhat; I hear they have moved back into northern Wisconsin. Most of these wolves keep to the deep woods but a few get into the bordering farmlands and kill livestock. The stockmen are *prohibited* from protecting their animals from wolves. More importantly, they are *not compensated* for the loss. In theory the rogue is promptly trapped by the proper authorities and either killed or removed to another area, but the dead sheep or cow or horse is still red ink. Not surprisingly, stockmen in northern Minnesota are not fond of Timber Wolves and even less fond of the "Feds" who protect them. Take my word for it (I used to get around up there), a lot of Timber Wolves are killed by the locals every year and left where they fall. Possession being nine-tenths of the law, an arrest is rare. The impetus for the killings more than anything else is spite.

The rationale of federal and state programs that subsidize the killing of unprotected predators which the rancher could and should take responsibility for himself, while failing to compensate the stockman's loss to a protected predator where his hands are legally tied, is difficult to fathom. A different approach is necessary if we ever hope to regain the wolf and

grizzly in New Mexico. Herein, a modest proposal comes to mind.

As a preliminary, it would be helpful if ranchers and conservationists would come to realize they have some common ground. As it stands, ranchers tend to think that all conservationists are "cement pounders;" city people whose occasional weekend excursions into the great outdoors don't qualify their raucous input on wilderness and wildlife issues. The conservationist, on the other hand, views today's rancher as an overgrazer on welfare, a group whose rugged individualism is only a memory; its members benefiting from a variety of federal subsidies, favoritism, and old-line political power out of all proportion to their numbers. Perhaps each side has a point. But a bigger point is that both sides, as they are composed of people who, whatever their differences, love the out-of-doors, have a stake in preserving what's left of the natural world from the onslaught of human overpopulation. When a rancher or farmer goes under, or willingly sells out, there is often a developer, a city, or some other aspect of the growth-at-all-costs philosophy ready to pick up the land or the water right and convert the agricultural land and wildlife habitat into subdivisions, tract homes, aggrandizing industrialization and other manifestations of urban blight. According to the U. S. Department of Agriculture, about *three million acres* of agricultural land is lost in this country each year...not to erosion, not to overgrazing, not to the machinations of the environmental community, but to urban and industrial growth. And I've often wondered if the American farmer/rancher is even remotely aware who the enemy really is. I regularly read several farm/ranch periodicals published here in the Southwest. The enemy, according to these folks, is: "...those damn

environmentalists and we're not going to take it anymore!"
Meanwhile, the developers are eating their lunch to the tune of
three million acres a year. On the other side of the fence,
environmentalists are equally misguided. "It's those damn
ranchers," they'll say, "get livestock off public lands!"
Meanwhile, the developers, the boomers and the boosters, are
eating *their* lunch! I'm an activist environmentalist and I like
farming and ranching. I'll take a chile field, an apple orchard,
permanent pasture or range land to a trailer park, subdivision
or shopping mall any day. Sure, a lot of the Western
rangelands are overgrazed. But many healthy rangelands can
be found, supporting all of habitat, livestock, and wildlife in
self-sustaining ecosystems. The solution some environmental
people have come up with is to try and raise the grazing fee on
public lands in hopes that the rancher won't be able to make the
payment and will belly up or abandon the range. I suspect this
will not cause the rancher to belly up or abandon the range but
will cause him to try and overstock the lease in an attempt to
make up for the fee increase. Raising the lease will certainly
make it tougher on the rancher but it won't necessarily improve
the range. My thought is not to stop grazing on public lands but
to stop *over*grazing, and the way to do that would be through a
Conservation Reserve Program (CRP) for rangeland. Just as
we pay farmers not to farm eroded lands, so they can recover,
we could pay ranchers to let overgrazed pastures lie fallow.
Take the cows off for awhile; when the range recovers restock
in sustainable numbers. Would that be another subsidy for
agriculture? You could call it that. So what? We subsidize most
everybody in this country. Poor folks in the inner cities are
subsidized. Reservation Indians are subsidized. Peanut and
dairy farmers are subsidized. Water developers and large

corporations are subsidized. Even some writers are subsidized! A subsidy is bad only if it's money wasted. The CRP is a subsidy and an enormously successful one, heartily endorsed by agriculture and conservation alike; it's done a world of good for wildlife and for agricultural land in the Midwest; it could do as well in the Southwest.

If the farm/ranch folks and the conservationists were not so culturally disparate they would have a common cause and could achieve much together in restraining or at least mitigating urban/industrial growth through some needed legislation, like the CRP, and through creative planning and zoning, that would preserve farm and ranch land, open space, wildlife and habitat all in a swoop.

I like ranching in particular. The rancher, and traditional ranch life, has much in common with the wolf and the grizzly and the wilderness; all are remnants of the frontier and part of American culture worth preserving, regardless of the economic bottom line. Since wolves and grizzlies do kill livestock, the logical compromise is for these animals to be given preference in a few remote regions better suited to wolves and bears, than to cattle and sheep. The logical place in New Mexico for the reintroduction of the Mexican Wolf and Grizzly Bear is the Gila National Forest. This is easily the most remote region within the state and, unlike the White Sands Missile Range, the currently proposed wolf introduction site, was the natural home of the Southwestern wolf and grizzly. The releases would be made within the Gila and Aldo Leopold Wilderness areas. Barring an incorrigible rogue endangering human life, the critters would receive total protection within designated wilderness. The remaining livestock leases within these areas could and should be phased out. Any wolf or bear

34

that got out of the wilderness and got into trouble would be subject to controls (killed or removed) by federal or state personnel and the loss or damage compensated. Once their numbers reached the point where a change in management was in order, a controlled hunting season for the big predators could be established.

Who would pay for such introductions? Who would provide funds for compensation? The New Mexico Department of Game & Fish has found money to introduce exotic species like Oryx, Ibex and Barbary Sheep. It spends vast sums and man-hours trying to keep the Mexican Bighorn Sheep herd alive, despite the fact the species seems at times determined to give up the ghost. These species aren't obviously destructive and so not too controversial, but they are certainly costly in their way. If these animals are worth both the time and money, certainly wolves and grizzlies should draw similar professional interest. If the "Feds" can establish an endangered species program they can fund the compensation to help make the program work. And all that government subsidy handed out for such things as trapping coyotes in June (when the hides are worthless) and poisoning prairie dogs *et al,* ought to go to endangered animals. The Audubon Society currently offers a $10,000 reward for information leading to the conviction of any grizzly poacher. These and other private sources are possibilities for funds as well.

It is hard to define the essence of what was lost when the grizzly and the wolf left the Southwest. If you've ever seen one in the wild, you know. I have never seen a grizzly in the wild but I have seen wolves and one time in Minnesota I got a run at one.

35

On deep snow I put two hounds down on a coyote track in below zero weather. They took the track across a field then, just shy of the woods, left it for a second track that crossed over. That would mean two coyotes traveling together; I didn't care which one they ran.

They jumped the second one and for five minutes we had a frantic yelping, bawling race...then silence. Five minutes after that here they come back to the truck, on the run. I can read expressions in my own hound's faces. These two looked just plain silly, and embarrassed. Like a couple of sheep killing dogs, or trash-running hounds. I said, "You sons-a-bitches!" (what else do you say to a couple of sorry hounds?) and I loaded them up.

Down the road I saw where that second track crossed and I got out to see if they'd left a coyote track to run a buck or a doe. It looked like a St. Bernard had crossed the road.

I can see still see that wolf back in there; how he ran, then stopped, waited, then lunged, popping his teeth, sending two veteran coyote killers scrambling back to the truck, looking silly.

Another time in Minnesota I was with a friend checking his coyote traps and we came to where a coyote with enormous feet had tripped the set and run off with the trap and the drag. We followed to where the drag had hung the critter up in some alder brush. We were too late to save him, as his foot was ruined, but he was still alive, must have weighed near one hundred pounds, and he was mad. While we watched and considered what to do he snapped in a rage at that alder brush. It was green saplings of alder, some of the toughest stuff that grows, and some of them were as big around as your thumb and that wolf clipped those saplings off like a brush cutter. It was

36

enthralling and very impressive and, to be sure, more than a little bit sad.

I once saw where a Black Bear had taken down a Hereford twice his size, the brush tore up all around, and how he peeled back the hide as he ate, busting bones along the way. But that's not a grizzly. That's maybe three hundred pounds.

Montague Stevens, a one-armed Englishman with tough horses and a hound pack, knew the grizzly in southwest New Mexico. He wrote it all up in *Meet Mr. Grizzly*. He packed his grizzlies out piece by piece and then weighed the bloodless carcass and the hide. He thus could report with authority that the largest southwestern grizzlies weighed at or near "eight hundred pounds." Good Christ! That's a bear that could pull stumps with a roll of his paw.

Leopold knew such a bear well, still in the Sierra del Gila, just across the New Mexico line near Springerville, Arizona. He wrote of the last grizzly of Escudilla Mountain:

> *Old Bigfoot was a robber-baron, and Escudilla was his castle. Each spring, when the warm winds had softened the shadows on the snow, the old grizzly crawled out of his hibernation den in the rock slides and, descending the mountain, bashed in the head of a cow. Eating his fill, he climbed back to his crags and there summered peaceably on marmots, conies, berries and roots.*
>
> *I once saw one of his kills. The cow's skull and neck were pulp, as if she had collided head-on with a fast freight.*

SIERRA DEL GILA

What was lost, in each case, was a singular magnificence. Could there be a more noble effort than to restore magnificence to the last great wilderness in the Southwest?

~ ~ ~ ~ ~ ~

Good morning, Rojo! I awake to find a well-furred canine sleeping on my feet. He's dead to the world and so is my left foot.

A sip of *Southern Comfort* never hurt anyone, but the better part of a pint will put you away. By the time I had crawled into my tent by the melodious waters of Iron Creek I was really in the wilderness. Following Rojo out of the tent the next morning I was blessed by a blue sky. Very chill air - a light frost - also aided my revival; the sun was still behind the hills. I carried a numb left foot, by hopping on the right one, over to the icy flow of Iron Creek and, kneeling, splashed water on my face. That helped too.

With vision and circulation returning to normal I rigged up my stubby little spinning rod. No class, I hoped to catch a wilderness trout on a tiny hook baited with salmon eggs.

I am not a good trout fisherman, have never attained skill or proper respect for the sport. I have caught the usual varieties (Browns, Rainbows, Brook and Lake Trout) in a number of states. I have used everything from worms to the most arcane dry fly. Fishing writers (and writers who fish) that I have the utmost respect for continue to inspire me with their words on the subtleties and nuances of the elegant outdoor pursuit of fly fishing, but once at the water and given the choice I'll still take bait or a lure and Smallmouth Bass, or Northern Pike, or best of all - catfish! On Iron Creek there are only Brown Trout and the native Gila Trout. The Gila Trout is protected - you're supposed to throw them back - but neither was in any danger from me that morning. I got nary a nibble but I did manage to scare a few off. In an hour or so I walked back to camp, added water to a cup full of granola and blueberries and submitted to breakfast. Afterwards I crouched by the fire for a while surrounding a cup of coffee. Seeing a warm patch of sun creeping into a place between the pines I crawled over there and went to sleep.

Sometime later that morning Rojo stuck a wet nose in my ear and - just as well - woke me up. I threw my outfit together and started down the trail along the creek. With the sun now well up I became aware of how absolutely lucid the water was: where the current was slack it looked like you could touch the stones on the bottom without getting your hand wet. Here and there a wild rose had begun to flower. And there was Ponderosa and some oak on the left side of the stream and spruce and fir on the right as distinct as if the forestry boys had planted them that way. The rainfall did not vary within a distance of a stone's throw; it was the varying effects of shading that altered the botany in that peculiar manner. In the high country of the Gila Forest, especially along the creeks and canyons, such demarcations are obvious. And where the creek or canyon changes direction the biome will that quickly change sides. Juxtaposition, contrast, along Iron Creek. I liked it.

After a while - a mile or two - the trail cut across the creek and started uphill on the other side. I checked the map and saw that this trail directed one through something called the Clayton Mesa. After several miles it looked to come to the Gila just below Iron Creek. Down Iron Creek itself there was no more trail but there were a lot of blowdowns I'd have to climb over and around. Thinking I was probably in too much of a hurry I nonetheless crossed the creek and took the shortcut to the Gila.

It was a steep climb up to the Clayton Mesa but an easy walk from there across the flat which had Ponderosa scattered around and once again reminded me of a park. The country looked drier than what I'd been seeing. About halfway across we surprised a flock of wild turkeys, several grown ones and a bunch of poults. Rojo made a swift pass, a big circle, around the flock and came back well pleased, seeming to know how far he could go without getting his ass kicked. Soon I set the pack down on the rim of a rock drop off overlooking the Gila River. The trail sign anticipating the way down said: *"Not recommended for horses or livestock."*

On bear and lion chases I've taken horses off worse places than that but there were areas where you might want to get off and lead. As it was, on foot and top-heavy, I slipped down solidly on my butt several times. I didn't enjoy that. I did enjoy finally getting there whence I dropped my pack, stood in the water and drank. With the waters of Snow Creek, Iron Creek, Gilita Creek, Willow Creek and maybe a few others added in, this was altogether a pretty good stream. This was the Gila, Middle Fork.

As you walk down the Middle Fork of the Gila River you encounter canyon walls, rock walls, bluffs, and where you do, you have to cross to the other side. "Bluffed up" I guess is the phrase. One thing I planned right was to wear tennis shoes. Crossing every quarter to half mile the water was cool but not real cold, still real clear and seldom over my knees. I promptly picked up a staff, a walking stick, and with the added control and the right foot gear I was able to shuffle across the slick, rocky bottom without falling in. Rojo enjoyed the crossings (he

41

hit 'em all on the run) and in places he got to swim. He swims better than most hounds, enjoys the water more than most hounds, but in no case is he a water dog like the several Labrador Retrievers I've owned in the past.

Riparian vegetation is the plant growth that appears along perennial streams in the Southwest. Cottonwood, willow, sycamore and tamarisk (an exotic) are the common trees along the Gila. Along Iron Creek I hadn't seen any of these trees but I'd lost enough altitude - at least 4,000 feet since Hummingbird Saddle - that cottonwood and sycamore were now showing up adjacent to the water. Pine, Gambel's Oak and Alligator Juniper were scattered around and there were still a few fir trees in certain shaded areas. There was a lot of piñon, a drought resistant pine, on the sunny slopes. I guess you'd call it *Transition* Zone but it was an astounding variety of vegetation right there along the upper Middle Fork. Fir trees, which seemingly belonged back at Whitewater Baldy, would disappear before long, while the cottonwoods would be with me through journey's end in Arizona. For the moment I had it all right there.

I set my pack down underneath a cottonwood to try to ease once more certain knots of muscle. Right there was a small, green pool, rather deep, by a rock wall with a little riffle leading away downstream. I put a small spinner on and made a number of casts into and through that pool and then down and back up through the fast water. I didn't catch anything but got a couple of follows from small trout. Shouldering my pack once again I flushed a husky Cottontail Rabbit from under a nearby blowdown - she'd been there all along and evidently could stand the suspense no longer. The rabbit made across this little glade in long lively leaps for the brush in a little header canyon...but she didn't make it. With a remarkable display of speed and athletic élan the hound picked her up on the run. He brought her back still kicking. I rapped her head against the cottonwood. Then I peeled her hide, dressed her out, cut off the head and feet and washed the carcass clean and cool in the stream. I pulled a large, red bandanna out of my back pocket, soaked it cool, and wrapped the rabbit inside. I tucked it all away in the pack.

About an hour down the river I saw a cave in a rock wall on the far side of the Gila. It had evidently been carved out over the eons by high water. This cave was now several feet above the waterline and the lip formed a nice porch. There was a rock fireplace ready-made inside and some dry wood piled up; this was evidently a popular place to camp. There wasn't anyone there though - I hadn't seen a soul in days. Even before I crossed over I saw this cave as a place that Ben Lilly had used many times, the perfect place to hood up till the rain stopped, the blizzard went by, or the lion tracks warmed up. I said, "Rojo, that's Ben Lilly Cave." Rojo cleared the stream in two jumps and beat me over there.

Ben Lilly Cave is a lovely place to stretch out on the bedroll just out of reach of a slow evening rain you can barely hear and take a nap. In retrospect it's hard to justify a long nap in what's billed as a wilderness adventure, but when things come easy on a good day you take it as is. I had natural shelter, a sand floor to sleep on, dry wood provided by the kindly, and a rabbit awaiting suppertime.

Not long before the sun went down I woke up; I sat on the edge of the *portal*, the porch, of Ben Lilly Cave and watched its colors disappear. Then, by the light of fire, I commenced preparations for a proper meal.

I was wanting rabbit stew but lacking flour, carrots and onions I was going to have to improvise. I did have two large potatoes. A potato is a good thing to bring along on a back-packing trip. It'll keep, it doesn't take up much room, the pulp is filling and the skin nutritious. Most of all it adds variety and savor to the usual freeze-dried menu. I also had a small plastic dish containing shortening and a little sack of corn meal. This was in anticipation of fish. I don't know of any tradition of corn meal with rabbit but I nonetheless doused cutup rabbit in corn meal and lay it and the slices from one potato in hot grease. In a saucepan I worked up a double order of freeze-dried beef stew. After a while I put the rabbit, grease and potato in with the stew, a bit of salt and pepper, and simmered it all till I couldn't stand it any longer. Thanks mostly to the rabbit the unlikely concoction yielded, somehow, an old-fashioned "Hunter's Stew." It was reminiscent of favored meals years ago, when my mother and/or aunt used to spoil my cousin and me after we'd come into the kitchen from a successful hunt laden down with partridge, Cottontail Rabbit and sometimes Snowshoe Hare. I mixed a quantity in with dry dog kibble for the great Rojo and, altogether, we done good.

I cannot imagine camping without a fire in the evening. There are times to be sure when a drenching rain make this impossible, but the current enthusiasm for camp stoves on the grounds that the use of natural fuel is an unsavory human imposition on the environment is an argument I'll walk around as long as I can find dead wood. I carried no camp stove; I did not want to be tempted to use it. Instead I got a blazer going there at Ben Lilly Cave. For obvious reasons I wasn't a bit sleepy. I sat up against the rock wall of this cave and let the flames back up the chill. This is precisely how ol' Ben survived winter nights in the Gila, sitting up by the fire, dozing off then stoking it up, the hounds packed in around him like so many warm bedmates. It wasn't nearly that cold on this spring night; indeed the system worked well enough that I was soon inching down the wall, keeping the pleasure of warmth at a proper distance. I left my bottle of *Southern Comfort* alone, finding the right comfort with coffee and a pipe. Off to the side Rojo received the fire's highlights but not its warmth; with his coat of hair he could afford to keep more distance than I. Though catching rabbits was not what he was bred and raised to do - it doesn't rank with a cougar chase, or bear chase or even a coyote chase - I was nonetheless pleased with the boy. His presence fit the scene...I had found Ben Lilly's tracks.

My journey down the Gila was not a hunting trip; it was the wrong time of year for most game animals. I intended to do little hunting but a good deal of fishing. Of course one could argue, as I often do, that fishing is hunting; it's the way in which one hunts fish. On this day Rojo and I had caught, killed and eaten a rabbit. I'm no more vegetarian than him; for the both of us on that good day, good memories were formed for all our time, highlighted, of course, by the chase, the catch and the meal. It all seemed natural enough to me, and I would have to assume for Rojo as well. But I'm coming to learn all that bothers some people. Some of these folks are out on the fringe and are not to be helped. No matter what you kill, or why or how you kill it, they are going to object. If the final result is meat on the table, or a hide on the wall, or a fur or leather somebody uses as clothes, they're going into a lather that will not be assuaged pending a set of laws outlawing death. Yet there are others, more numerous, who have objections that are not so easily dismissed.

~ ~ ~ ~ ~ ~

One with strong conservationist leanings who spends most of his days afield attempting to kill something often finds himself on guard at both flanks. It's safe to say that a majority of those who are most adamant about preserving or expanding wilderness areas, salvaging endangered species and maintaining free-running rivers in their natural state, are not enthusiastic about the "consumptive" outdoor pursuits. Some are frankly opposed. They think you're a great guy until they walk into your house one day and find a coyote hide strung out over a stretcher, or hear about how, the year before, the two Greyhounds and one Saluki out in the yard caught fifty jackrabbits. Conversely, there is the modern hunter. With apologies ahead of time to the exceptions, he doesn't operate far from his vehicle or the road it relies on; he's more intrigued by ballistics than his own shooting skill; more concerned with "good access" into wildlife habitat than with saving wildlife habitat. The extreme concern many modern hunters carry for "good access" is born out each year at the annual meeting of the National Rifle Association, an outfit that does a good job of protecting the rights of gun owners and which always gets my yearly membership dues. As an annual ritual, the NRA leadership votes in support of increased multiple use of public lands and in specific opposition to wilderness protection. The reason given is that wilderness is inimical to wildlife management. This, of course, is so much stuff and feathers. Wildlife management and wilderness management are quite compatible, and a variety of trophy game continues to come out of wilderness lands. The NRA leadership doesn't like wilderness because you can't drive around in there; "good access" therein is limited to those who are willing to walk or ride a horse. Ben Lilly, last of the mountain men and a legend in the Southwest and to those anywhere who have ever hunted with a hound, was a wilderness lover who had little use for the modern precepts of conservation. As a hunter he was in a class by himself. He did it right. But in many ways he had it all wrong. As a delineator and definer of the above debate and issues, he's worth a look.

Ben Lilly was the greatest houndman who ever lived. This can't be proved of course and you could form another opinion by pointing to several people who may have killed more bear and lion in a career. From reading J. Frank Dobie's fine book, *The Ben Lilly Legend*, one can figure up that Ben Lilly in his lifetime killed about six hundred mountain lions and close to five hundred bears. Along the Blue River, Arizona, I once met the late Clell Lee, another legend in his time. He and his brother Dale came into their own as houndmen about the time Ben Lilly was packing it in, fading into a benign senility. Clell Lee made us each a sandwich, poured coffee, introduced me to his hounds and told me that during his career, hunting mostly in Arizona and New Mexico, he had taken "at least six hundred bear and more lions than that." He did not impress me as a man with any need to tell a stretcher. In the swamps and humid woods of Mississippi, Louisiana, and East Texas, Ben Lilly spent the first fifty years of his life and accounted for 120 bears and, at best, half as many lions. In the latter half of the nineteenth century these creatures were already nearing extinction in the South. In his twenty years of hunting in southwest New Mexico and adjacent range in Arizona (1911 to about 1930) Ben Lilly averaged some twenty bears and thirty lions per year. Where other hunters lived at a ranch and made excursions into the wilderness with their dogs, Lilly lived in the wilderness, making occasional excursions to a ranch or base camp for fresh dogs and supplies. His adventures in the wild, and exploits and eccentricities, created stories based on fact, and legends and lore, much of which Dobie collected and wrote well of in his book. I read the book, and over the years read the recollections of others who had known Lilly, but I wasn't content with the reading. What I wanted to do was talk to someone who had known Lilly, and who had actually hunted with him. By the time I arrived in Southwest New Mexico in 1980, such remnants of the frontier were scarce, an endangered species about to fade forever from the scene. Time after time, one old timer or another would tell me, "No, I didn't know him, but I saw him a time or two, when he'd come into town." Or, "No, I never hunted with Ben Lilly, but I knew him some; talked to him several times at the county poor farm where he went after he got senile." That wasn't what I wanted. Then I met Jack Hooker, well into his eighties but still lucid and interested in life. He and his wife had recently retired from their ranch and had come to a little place outside Silver City to watch what was left in life go by. Mrs. Hooker poured coffee and Jack Hooker started to talk and for the next hour I had my living link to the last of the mountain men...

"Yea, I hunted with him; I knew Ben Lilly pretty good. I'd ride and he'd walk alongside as fast as any horse and he'd talk faster than that. Talk all day. He'd have half a dozen hounds anyway, and he didn't tie his dogs; they obeyed him. When the race would start and go to rough country, you couldn't keep up with him. The first time I went with Ben Lilly I went afoot, like him. That was a mistake. I was in my twenties then, and he was past sixty, but when the race started and the hounds went over the mountain, Lilly walked me down.

He lost me. After that I rode a horse when I hunted with Ben Lilly."

Hooker also remembered Lilly's artistic talents.

"He was an artist. He was always making hunting horns to call his hounds in. With the point of his knife he would mark out little dots on the horn that would come out a bear or lion. Beautiful work. And he could make a knife overnight, right there in camp. Made them out of a trap spring, tempered in a campfire, always sharpened on both sides. I gave all my Lilly knives away over the years. I wish I had one now to show you. He was an artist with a knife."

Jack Hooker recalled that Lilly's favorite camp in the Gila Wilderness was a cave about a mile up Sapillo Creek from its junction with the main Gila.

"I was little more than a boy. We were working cattle along the Sapillo and camped along the Gila. Ben Lilly would come down to our camp now and again, talk a blue streak whether you answered back or not, then disappear. In a blizzard one day down there we lost our horses. Myself and some other boys found some of Ben Lilly's burros. He always had real nice burros to help him move camp. We had to get out of that blizzard so we rode his burros into Silver City and a deputy took us in for stealing Ben Lilly's burros. He put the burros in the pound. Later, Ben Lilly walked in from the Sapillo to get his burros. He told the sheriff to let us go; he didn't care if we borrowed his burros, blizzard or not. That deputy was going to make a name for himself catching us with Ben Lilly's burros, but he didn't get it done. We boys thought Ben Lilly was alright."

Later Jack Hooker had his own ranch along the nearby Mimbres River. Along with other ranchers in the area, he paid

Ben Lilly $100 per lion as bounty. In *The Ben Lilly Legend*, J. Frank Dobie wrote that by 1928 Ben Lilly had "ceased to be very active." Jack Hooker remembers things differently.

"Hell, he got five lions in one month off our ranch alone in 1929. That was too much; no lion was worth $100 in 1929. That was an awful lot of money then. The last one was the worst. The deal was, whoever had the ranch where the lion was killed, he paid the bounty. One day Ben's dogs treed a lion on a neighbor's ranch. Ben shot the lion but only wounded it. It baled out and ran a good ways before they treed it again. That second tree was on our ranch. Ben killed the lion out of that second tree, so we owed him the hundred dollars. That was too much. We let Ben go and I started to build my own pack. Used some of Ben's dogs, too."

Jack Hooker told me that lion hunting had changed since Ben Lilly's time.

"Nowdays a lion hunter may have a four-wheel drive truck and a snowmobile to help catch a lion. That's not how Lilly did it. You don't learn about lions or hunting, driving around. Ben Lilly was the best because he was at home in the wilds, as much as any hound or varmint."

After Ben Lilly was gone, Jack Hooker remembered his cave along Sapillo Creek.

"I knew he had buried something just outside the mouth of that cave. I always wondered what it was - a knife maybe, money? I was down there one time and I dug it up. It was the grave of one of his best hounds, ever. He buried Crook there and on the lid of a shoebox in pencil he wrote this out."

Jack Hooker handed me the cover of the shoe box. You could still read it. In long hand, more elegant than grammatical, Lilly had written:

*Here lies Crook, a bear and lion dog
that helped kill 210 bear and 426 lion
since 1914 owned by B. V. Lilly. He
died here the first Tuesday night in
February 1925. He was owned and
raised in camp and died in camp here.
B. V. Lilly February 1925.*

Ben Lilly at the height of his powers, with Crook and his other
hounds, had killed 210 bear and 426 lion over a span of eleven
years. Had he begun and maintained his hunting in this same
range his numbers would have been untouchable.

But what Ben Lilly could do as a hunter cannot be seen
in the numbers. Like anyone who has achieved greatness with
hunting dogs, he knew, intuitively and without knowledge of
genetics, how to coalesce and work bloodlines to produce pup-
pies with instincts for the chase. The Lilly dogs were fast,
toughfooted, gritty, coldnosed and with the treeing ability to
stay with any game that climbed. The Lilly dogs would literally
"starve at the tree." To this day in southwest New Mexico
hunters will claim that their hounds are descended from the
Lilly dogs. Much of this is wishful thinking but the wish trib-
utes the man. Other hunters, I suspect, have produced individual hounds of the quality of the Lilly dogs. No one ever spent
more time afield in company with the pack. No hunter before
or since had Ben Lilly's capacity for reading sign, nor his endurance and perseverance on the trail. Ben Lilly and his
hounds lost trails to wind, blizzards and baking sun; it is
doubtful if they ever quit one in response to hunger, thirst or
exhaustion. Not even with a gun at your head could you ever

SIERRA DEL GILA

hunt as hard as Ben Lilly. The only thing that can cause that kind of primal single-mindedness is a congenital enthusiasm for the chase. All houndmen have it to a degree. Ben Lilly had it in equal measure with his own hounds. The result was a man who would under the most adverse conditions catch a Black Bear, Grizzly or Mountain Lion that no one else could. No less an authority than Theodore Roosevelt (would that we could have a President today who knew and appreciated the natural world as Roosevelt!) was impressed by Lilly's talents in the wild. In 1907 Lilly served as Chief Huntsman to Roosevelt during a Presidential bear hunt in the Tensas Bayou of Louisiana. Later, Roosevelt would describe Lilly as "...spare, full bearded, with mild, gentle, blue eyes and a frame of steel and whipcord. I never met any other man so indifferent to fatigue and hardship. He equaled Cooper's Deerslayer in woodcraft, in hardihood, in simplicity - and also in loquacity. The morning he joined us in camp, he had come on foot through the thick woods, followed by his two dogs, and had neither eaten nor drunk for twenty-four hours; for he did not like to drink the swamp water. It had rained hard throughout the night and he had no shelter, no rubber coat, nothing but the clothes he was wearing, and the ground was too wet for him to lie on; so he perched in a crooked tree in the beating rain, much as if he had been a wild turkey. But he was not in the least tired when he struck camp; and, though he slept an hour after breakfast, it was chiefly because he had nothing else to do, inasmuch as it was Sunday, on which day he never hunted or labored. He could run through the woods like a buck, was far more enduring, and quite as indifferent to weather, though he was over fifty years old. He had trapped and hunted throughout almost all the half century of his life, and on trail of game he was as sure as his own hounds. His observations on wild creatures were singularly close and accurate..." There is certainly a heroism of sorts attendant to such outdoor skills. From a modern perspective this heroism is tainted by the man's lack of foresight regarding just exactly what he was doing.

"With renewed assurance of his mission in life," Dobie wrote, "the lover of the wild went on annihilating it." Ben Lilly had a large hand in the extirpation of the Grizzly from the Southwest. If he was ever bothered by this thought it isn't evident in the writings from or about the man. He wasn't a cattleman. Hunting out of a pure and consuming instinct, one would think that even as a practical matter he would want to preserve the species if for no other reason than to have one to hunt now and again. The efficiency with which he cleared out particular mountain ranges of Black Bear and lion evidences the same passion for destruction.

The Black Bear in New Mexico received some protection in the form of game regulations even in Ben Lilly's time. It took a while for the same thinking to reach the cougar, but today its population as well is carefully monitored. It is estimated that today there are some 1,000 to 2,000 Mountain Lions in New Mexico and 3,000 to 4,000 Black Bear. Arizona has at least that many lions; nearly as many bear. For each animal, in each state, regulations keep the yearly kill under 20 percent of the total population. Similar regulations protect the bear and lion in all the western states except (where else?) Texas. Neither species is in any danger of extermination in the West, but a look at the hunting of these animals says a lot about how the modern hunter has evolved since Ben Lilly's time.

In those states where it's legal (in New Mexico it's not, in Arizona it still is although, apparently, they're phasing it out) the most popular method of bear hunting is baiting. This requires the hunter (or guide) to truck a barrel of fish guts, or a dead horse, or other delectable to the woods, park himself in a blind nearby and, provided he doesn't fall asleep, shoot the ignorant bruin as he comes into the meal. The sport requires little knowledge of the outdoors or ability to survive in the wild, no physical endurance or risk, no knowledge of horse or hunting dog, no ability to read sign. It requires, in short, none of the skills one thinks of as being part of the hunting experience. It isn't even necessary to find the bear; the bear finds you.

In contrast, attempting a bear with a pack of hounds is one of the most demanding outdoor sports. You have to find the bear, or at least his track, and that takes time. Your hounds will be as good as the breeding and training you have put into them. The chase, usually, goes on for hours, over the most rugged terrain the bear can find; many bear refuse to tree. If you don't hustle you lose the dogs. It is rare that one of the dogs is not injured by the bear. It is not unusual for one to be killed. If you're afoot you'll be on your back, gasping for mercy, half way up the first mountain while the sound of your hounds in pursuit carries on to parts unknown. Horseback, you'd better be ready if your horse goes down, or peels you off in the brush. You climb back up, bite your lip and go on. There is seldom danger to the hunter from the bear itself; there is danger enough without it. Should the bear be forced to tree or bay up, and should you choose to kill it, you pack the animal out, a considerable chore in itself in that he's likely many miles from the nearest road. But the meat is fine, the hide of value, and win or lose, if you're gripped by the atavism of the chase you call it good. If you're not, this is merely a very brutal business. It is that in any event, with all involved - horse, hound, bear and hunter - jerked down to a physical essence.

The Mountain Lion, because he likes fresh meat, is not vulnerable to the baiting approach. Still, the sport has been corrupted. The ruination of modern lion hunting (the ruin of modern hunting generally) is the four-wheel drive vehicle. The old style lion hunt - horses, hounds, hunters camped out, riding from can to can't till cutting a lion track, staying on that cold track till the lion is jumped hot and treed - is on the way out, though it's better maintained in the Southwest than anywhere else. Increasingly, the modern lion hunter waits till the snow falls, then drives the back roads till he finds a track. Instead of covering ten to twenty miles a day he manages one to two hundred. He can afford to pass up the older, colder track, which would require a lot of time and effort for the hounds and hunter to work out; he drives on till he finds a fresh track. The result, usually, is a short chase and a treed lion, for the cougar has little endurance (albeit great speed) and even less courage once the hounds are in close pursuit. Most of the time spent "hunting," the participants are sitting behind a windshield, drinking coffee, listening to the radio and talking on the CB. This approach is especially prevalent where a hunter takes a dude on a guided hunt, for often the client is averse to cross-country work, afoot or horseback.

Many who have treed lots of lions have never seen one unattended in the wild. As a bear or lion hunter, I have mostly just tagged along, but I have seen a lion on the loose, by happenstance, in south Texas.

We were riding fence along the Nueces River in Mc-Mullen County. My horse suddenly set the back of his head up against my chest, attempting to focus on something with his nostrils. Nobody saw him until he moved, though he wasn't twenty yards away; and then he cleared a small meadow in the mesquite brush in two remarkable bounds and was gone. The old man I was riding with had worked this ranch all his life, had seen lion tracks and lion kills all his life but, like me, this was his first sight of the lion. Possibly the most secretive, elusive creature in the wilds. The hunting of him is a fascinating story involving canine detectives. A bear chase is a battle, a running fight. A coyote chase, where I have done most of my hunting on my own, is a race. Any of it will separate the men from the boys, the horses from the colts, the dogs from the pups.

Pursuit with hounds is of course only one approach to hunting. It has, as Leopold said, "real split-rail flavor." In England, to this day, "hunting" means being afield with hounds; all else is "gunning" or "shooting" or some other particular. A further comment from Leopold on the subject has it that, "hunting generally involves the handling of dogs and horses, and the lack of this experience is one of the most serious defects of our gasoline-driven civilization." But any form of hunting can be corrupted or tainted by method.

Predator calling has become enormously popular over the past twenty years. Indians and frontiersmen learned long ago that a reed or blade of grass could be blown to produce a squeak or squall, imitating the distress cry of a mouse or rabbit. A coyote, fox or other predator may be lured to within shooting distance. Mouth blown calls now come out of the factory and the imitation has been improved upon. It still takes skill to use one, however. But a fascination with gadgets soon brought us cassette tapes and loudspeakers. The cry of the dying rabbit is now *broadcast* into the wild. The improvement over the mouth blown call is slight, if there's any at all, but a gadget is alluring and many a predator hunter has discarded his mouthblown call as "old-fashioned."

Also over the past twenty years many a hunter has given up his rifle for a bow. This is a positive step in an era of diminishing habitat and hunting opportunities. The success rate with bow and arrow in deer hunting is less than half that achieved by rifle hunters. But what type of bow does the modern hunter use? Ninety percent have gone from the longbow or recurve to the compound bow, a contraption, to be blunt, involving wheels and levers. The muscle power required to pull a given bow weight is reduced and there's some increase in arrow speed. On the other hand a good longbowman is just as accurate and can loose his arrows faster. The compound bow is an innocuous contraption; any bow requires significant hunting skills for consistent success; my tribute goes out to any successful bowhunter. Here again it's a question of aesthetics. The longbow or recurve is an art form, in its making and its use; in aesthetic juxtaposition the compound is an eyesore.

More than forty years ago Aldo Leopold, typically prophetic, noted that the American sportsman now takes to the field "...with an infinity of contraptions, all offered as aids to self-reliance, hardihood, woodcraft or marksmanship, but too often functioning as substitutes for them." And what would Leopold say of the New-Age paraphernalia and mechanization the American sportsman takes to the woods and streams with today?

Restraints, self-restraints, are what the hunter today must place between himself and his game - some practical, some ethical, some aesthetic. The decisions regarding each are personal and necessarily arbitrary. I would not want the job of listing precisely what ought to be permissible. One thing is certain. Wild country, designated or otherwise, forces restraint upon any hunter, eliminates 90 percent of the serious abuses and invariably improves the venetic art aesthetically. The four-wheel drive vehicle is of no use to you in the Gila Wilderness, be you a hunter of Mountain Lions, Mule Deer or jackrabbits. Enter the Gila and you invite a physical workout. Certain risks are involved. Lacking certain skills, knowledge or at least common sense and you're looking to get lost, freeze to death, drown maybe, or break your foolish neck. One is required therein to focus closely on doing it right. A week in the wilderness will make an honest hunter out of an incorrigible cheat.

Which brings us back to those folks with objections. Again we discard the fringe, those people who won't and can't be pleased by all the rest of us living normal lives. The majority aren't out on the fringe, nor do they in our modern urban society hunt, trap or fish. For those of us who do hunt, trap or fish, they aren't the enemy...yet. But they are easily swayed by appearances.

Recently a special on network TV focused on a cougar study and within the hour-long show was a short sequence of a mountain lion hunt. A couple of Idaho hunters were only too happy to oblige the producers. So they all went out on camera: several hunters, a bunch of dogs, three four-wheel drives, a snowmobile, CB radios all around, and each dog had radio telemetry collars, which not only told the hunter where they were but also, by the change in the signal, told them when they had their heads up barking treed. This hunt did not take place in wilderness; with motorized mobility on the numerous snow-packed forest roads it didn't take them long to cut a fresh track. The hounds were released, were soon in full cry, and the hunters stood on the road, listening not so much to the sounds of the chase as to the beep in the telemetry receiver. When the hounds treed, they knew it; the beeper told them so. Then, at the tree after a short hike, the guided hunter wanted to use his handgun. You could tell the way he handled it he was a little bit afraid of it and, sure enough, while close enough to hit that lion in the head with a rock, he shot the critter in the hip. The lion came down and thrashed around until one of the guides made the one shot that should have come in the first place. The whole country had a good look at lion hunting at its worst and everyone from Cleveland Amory to Paul Harvey took a shot at it. Blame the TV folks? I think not. They no doubt enjoyed portraying something they don't approve of in a bad light, but it still took the modern hunter to provide the opportunity for the message.

What is lion hunting then, in proper form? Pick up a copy of *Western Life and Adventure in the Great Southwest* by Elliot Barker and read the chapter "Three Days on a Lion's Trail." Barker's account of one hunter, one horse and a few hounds in a wilderness pursuit lasting three days is in sharp contrast to the motorized safari the nation got to see. Barker's account is lion hunting. Too bad it's not on film; even someone out on the fringe could see the difference.

I'm saying that it's not enough just to obey the rules, that beyond seasons and bag limits, appearances count. In our time, with the majority poised to either approve or disapprove of the consumptive outdoor pursuits, appearances perhaps count more than anything. And the majority is reacting unfavorably, not so much to the fact that we occasionally take home meat or a hide, but to the way we go about it. They see road hunters. They see poachers and game hogs. They see sportsmen laden down with gadgets and a myriad of modern artificial supports, from trucks for "good access," to range finders to fish finders. They're turned off and in such a state the fringe folks little by little gather them in. When they get enough of them on their side of the fence, the pursuit itself will be history.

Today the impetus for outdoor pursuits is neither survival nor Ben Lilly's missionary zeal to kill. It's not the achievement so much as the attempt - how you go about it. The venetic pursuit is primal. It is not passive. Once you've killed - or even attempted to kill - you're involved in a way you'll never be picking blueberries, skiing the slopes, watching the birds, trekking the forest trails or climbing the big one because it's there. Game departments do well in controlling the numbers killed. The methods remain largely open, to choice and interpretation. The less artificial, contrived and mechanized the method, the closer one comes to the animal pursued, the less ambivalent one need feel when the blood, finally, is on your hands. One looks to an approach that is at once atavistic and restrained.

Curling up for sleep way late with a full belly and a hound at Ben Lilly Cave, I wonder by the fire if a tough, bearded old eccentric didn't come finally to a greater wisdom than the extant history has recorded. It is somehow more pleasant and hopeful to think so.

~ ~ ~ ~ ~ ~

A big chunk of oak, the last piece of wood I put on the fire, retained coals the next morning. Adding small twigs, I waved my stetson at the coals and pretty soon had a fire going. I cooked up leftovers and coffee, warmed some water and did the dishes. With the sparse aspects of my portable camp (for utensils I had a small teflon fry pan, a tin plate, a tin cup, a small saucepan, a fork, spoon and jackknife) this didn't take very long. While I was puttering around the camp a Tassel-eared Squirrel came down out of a big Ponderosa and began to forage around. Rojo promptly put him back up the tree. He spiraled up the trunk to a safe height, maybe ten feet, then turned upside down and with incessant chatter proceeded to tell that hound how and why.

I am very fond of the Tassel-eared (Abert's) Squirrel. A big one will go two pounds; only the Fox Squirrel is larger. The southwestern squirrel is more sporty however, faster on the ground and more agile in the tree. The noticeable black tufts on the tops of the ears contribute to a bizarre, exotic appearance. Down the back the fur is nearly black; in the fall sparse, rust-red guard hairs mingle with the dark. There's beauty in that and in the snow white belly and tail. They're savory. I had a .22 revolver in the pack and had it been squirrel season I no doubt would have tried to shoot this squirrel. I wouldn't knowingly shoot anything out of season. Not that I'm all that noble. It's mostly paranoia that keeps me honest - the guy that poaches game just that one time in his life is sure to get caught. I'd be marked for life.

I spent some time watching our Tassel-eared Squirrel, 'till he got bored teasing a hound and disappeared finally into the top branches of a ponderosa you couldn't get your arms around. They are a further example (it's hard to get away from this subject) of the splendidly variegated ecology of southwest New Mexico and adjacent range in southeast Arizona. Elk, Black Bear and Red Squirrels are at or near the southern limits of their range in the Gila country. Mexican animals, like the Javelina, Coatimundi and the White-sided (Antelope) Jackrabbits range northward into both states. The counterpart in trees are the Engelmann Spruce, Blue Spruce and aspen from the north, Chihuahua Pine and Apache Pine from the south. It's a marvelous blend of the Rocky Mountains and the Sierra Madre, with creatures like the Tassel-eared Squirrel and the Arizona Grey Squirrel particular to the southwestern states. The range of the Arizona Grey Squirrel is very particular. They are found mostly along the Blue and San Francisco Rivers. One could not be a traveler anywhere in the U.S. and find such a various, disparate, and yet harmonious ecology.

One could do worse than spend a day sitting at the *portal* of Ben Lilly Cave, watching squirrels and thinking about such things. But with the squirrel gone I crossed the stream with a pack on my back. *Vámonos Rojo!*

~ ~ ~ ~ ~ ~

Approaching a place on the map known as The Meadows, the canyon of the Middle Fork began to wall up impressively, one thousand feet and more. Way down below the height of cliffs two travelers took to chasing suckers.

That silly hound started it all. At each crossing suckers and sometimes trout lay in the shallows. They fled upstream at our approach. The trout simply disappeared - a shadowy flit - but the larger suckers were easily visible and Rojo would pursue the wake. The more he did this the better he liked it. He caught a hold of a couple of them but disliked the mouthful and they squirmed loose. But his enthusiasm eventually proved infectious. With a shout - *"Andele Rojo!"* - I dropped the pack and joined the chase. Working together we singled one out. Thrashing, splashing and falling all over the Gila, we got him corralled finally in the shallows and I scooped him out onto the bank. Nice sucker! Three maybe four pounds, he'd be firm-fleshed and good eating from a wilderness stream. But I rolled him back in. We chased another, then another - a bunch of them - beaching a second one finally, then setting him free. No small family would ever go hungry with a dog like Rojo around. Sucker chasing! Great sport that. The eastern-based outdoor magazines are missing something.

The Meadows opens up nicely from the canyon above and below, a hundred yards wide between the high bluffs. I set my pack down to rest, and to finish drying out. The Apaches would have sought The Meadows to camp with their horses and mules. Doubtless the early Spaniards did the same, and the later gringo trappers and prospectors, as well as moderns hunting elk, lion or deer, or just trail riding. It was easy enough to imagine them all, each with their own mounts, tack, garb and language, grateful for The Meadows; easier in fact than imagining a daydreamer in tennis shoes packing a green sack. Rojo took advantage of the open country to make some long circles, full of grace and rapid striding, for the sheer pleasure of running. He at least looked like he belonged.

On down, and abruptly me and Rojo were all in one frightened, thrilled and awed by the beauty of the Gila's natural world. An immense tom turkey, a real gobbler, came up out of the brush in big, frantic flight; he was flushed between me and the tall cliffs and so chose to fly rather than run. As he cackled and flapped aloft, here comes Rojo in full stride; he leapt supremely and sailed, clipping his teeth just below the ascending bird's tail feathers. As the turkey disappeared, a whir of wings brought us a small flock of Bandtail Pigeons, flushed out of a side canyon by the big bird. They sped toward us, a wonderful, colorful game bird, then flared away when they realized there was more than a turkey in their realm. Great stuff!

SIERRA DEL GILA

SIERRA DEL GILA

~ ~ ~ ~ ~ ~

I crossed and re-crossed the stream, leaning for rest on my staff and thinking that every side canyon should be explored and pictures taken. But I kept on. Not hurrying, but not stopping much either. Stepping through some brush into the stream to cross once more I met a fisherman - bit of a shock after not having seen anyone for three days. He was snapping a small gold spinner on and informed me that he'd already caught three trout. His partner downstream, he said, had done better on trout than him, and had also caught a nice Smallmouth Bass. In response to his query I remarked that I hadn't done that well, not specifying that in fact I'd done nothing at all - if you don't count suckers - and I didn't. Feeling foolish for neglecting traditional sport, wondering why after four days on the Gila I was still in such a damned hurry, I decided to stop at the first reasonable campsite and by golly catch a trout for supper.

Shortly, I found another cave to hood up in, smaller but still congenial and again with a sand floor. There was some nice water nearby; it looked promising for fish. Setting my pack down I met an old-timer riding an old plug and headed upstream. This was the partner. He was real chatty which in this case was all right because he'd lived in the area a good long while and had some interesting comments on historical matters. He also told me I'd likely catch something right there by the cave; it was a good pool and had been one of his regular stops over the years. Kindly, he left it to me and went on up around the bend.

I put a little pink flatfish on and went to work. There was a big boulder that set out in the middle of this pool and an old tree lying in the water adjacent; I tossed the lure in by the boulder and just under a limb and got a follow. I put it the same place again and had a fish on. He made a couple of nice, flashy little runs, then came gently to the beach, a 14-inch, red-speckled Brown Trout.

I put this pretty fish in a small pool of standing water next to the stream, then crossed the stream and sought fish from another angle. From the other side, the rock and sub-merged tree presented a different perspective. Casting under-hand, I lay the lure in there I thought just right. But on the re-trieve I snagged a little branch. I gave a jerk and the rod broke in half; I had evidently cracked the fiberglass in walking through the brush and once again in my life I was glad no one was around to witness my attempts at sport.

Back across the stream Rojo stood entranced, eyeing my slim catch. "Don't eat the fish, Rojo!" I began to unpack my camp. Directly, I heard the clip-clop of a horse at a good trot and looked up to see the ol' boy's mount coming my way, rider-less, and holding his nose a little to the side to keep the reins out from under his feet. Seeing me he broke off the trail to cross the stream. I yelled, "Whoa, you silly fool!" He stopped right there with his front feet in the Gila. This old horse did not impress me as an animal that would shake anyone loose from the saddle, but then a lot of horses that look like that have left a lot of people on the ground. I caught the reins and turned him around and was just about to step on and go see if everything was all right when the old gentleman came into view, well winded from walking so fast. He was very glad to see I had his horse. This being a rental animal from a local outfitter, he was headed for the barn, a good fifteen miles downstream and not a fence between to stop him. The man said he'd left him ground-tied when he stepped down to fish. "I didn't think he'd do it," he said, "but I think now he was waiting for that chance all day." I said, "Well at least you know he's not lost."

The old gentleman had had enough fishing for the day. After a while he rode off downstream towards his own camp. Shortly his friend followed. I bunched up a few rocks for a fireplace, cut up my second potato (a very large one), got a fire started and put the slices in hot grease. I gutted the trout, then lay the fish with his hide and head still on into corn meal and then into the pan. I could have used three or four his size but this wasn't bad at all. And better a Brown than a Rainbow.

As regards game fish, the Gila River had one to start with - the Gila Trout. These trout remind one of a Brown more than any other species, lacking however the red spots and often with yellowish fins. They were present from the high mountain tributaries like Iron Creek to the more warmish, silty water conditions down around Cliff. They were adaptable. They were not however, in game and fish parlance, "good competitors." When the Brown Trout was introduced into the Gila they out-hustled the Gila Trout for food, the Rainbows crossbred with them, and within a period of time those two had pretty well knocked the native species out of existence. Game & Fish and Gila Forest personnel got with it just in time and managed to sequester Gila Trout in pure form in certain of the smaller streams of the Gila drainage. The species appears now to be making a safe, if limited, recovery.

Meanwhile, the German Brown, not native to the U.S. anywhere, adapted well to the Gila. Like the Gila Trout they are tolerant of relatively warm, murky trout waters; more so than the Rainbow. Also better than the Rainbow, they thrive well on minnows and hellgrammites and other living things that come floating down the Gila, as well as insects. After the initial stockings were made little additional stocking was necessary. If you catch a Brown Trout in the Gila today you are catching a naturally reproducing, if not truly native, fish.

The Rainbow Trout is the darling of most trout fishermen, though purist trout fishermen seem to feel the Brown is smarter, tougher to catch; more of a challenge and more of a prize. Rainbows are regularly stocked in the Gila. There is some natural reproduction but it appears their numbers would be slim without the regular additions. I'm certainly not the only fisherman who would rather catch and eat a "natural" fish than a hatchery stocker. On the other hand, any Rainbow who's lived in the Gila long enough to reach a foot in length and attain pink-muscled meat has probably earned his keep.

There is evidence to indicate that the Gila River, even in the wilderness regions, is not as clean as it used to be. Livestock overgrazing is one culprit. It leads to a depletion of grass and second-growth, a faster run-off following rains and resultant silt. This has certainly been the case on the lower Gila, say from Mogollón Creek on down. Others before me, who know lots more about this sort of thing than I do, have suggested that grazing should be eliminated within the designated wilderness of the Gila. This should be accompanied by an allowance of natural fires to reduce the climax forest and promote grass and second-growth, a condition closer to the original. The result would be reduced run-off, less radical flooding, and a cleaner, cooler river providing a better natural reproduction environment for fish. Such a program would also provide a point of comparison with those areas of the Gila where livestock grazing continues. Good idea!

Three other game fish have been introduced into the Gila. All have done well on their own and are handsome additions: Smallmouth Black Bass, Channel Catfish and Flathead (a.k.a. Yellow, Mud, Opelousas) Catfish.

For years I fished for Smallmouth Bass in upstate New York and Canada. "Ounce for ounce and pound for pound," they say, "the gamest fish that swims." I've caught most species of fresh water fish; by my experience I'm inclined to agree. The smallmouth may achieve impressive size on the Gila; five pounders and better are possible and one to two pounders are a common size. There are few places in New Mexico where this great game fish can be found at all and the Gila is probably the best of these. They are becoming more plentiful; over a stretch of about sixty miles a good percentage of your catch will be these bass, on bait, lures or even flies. They are as lively, as handsome and as tasty as any I've caught elsewhere.

Thoughts on the greatly underrated catfish await the slightly warmer waters of the Gila below the East Fork Bridge when one is traveling by canoe.

~ ~ ~ ~ ~ ~

The flesh and crisp skin of fried trout peeled neatly off the bones in company of a sliced potato sizzled harsh and dark like chips was just right. I poured the grease and remnants over kibble and made a hound happy.

Evening came on and the narrow canyon rock walls loomed increasingly dark overhead, as if one were passing slowly into a great tunnel. In the slot above occasional stars formed in slow sequence. On slim ledges hundreds of feet off the ground scrub piñon and pine had established and maintained a stunted growth. Some grew nearly horizontal, seemingly out of mere fissure in rock. Such trees drew contemplation in the fading light. One wondered how they got there, how they got their start, and what sustained growth out of what

70

looked to be a solid rock face. The thought - fantasy really - was to climb up there, visit as unobtrusively as possible, spend the night perhaps, and see if there was not something to be learned in the company of such an arduous will to live. But fantasies aside, I am not a rock climber. And I was very tired. *"Mucho sueño, que no Rojo?"* But Rojo was way ahead of me. With the warm shoulder of a hound as pillow I, too, slept.

~ ~ ~ ~ ~ ~

About a mile below camp, traveling under an incredible ribbon of blue, though no sun yet (it is late morning before the sun lifts above the horizon provided by 1,000 foot canyon walls), I came upon my new friends from the day before. They were loading up their pack mule, preparing their own return to the wilds of civilization. Standing patiently - only because he was well tethered - nearby was an old horse who wanted very much to go home. After some congenial conversation I went on.

I began to encounter occupied campsites every mile or so. These were folks who had traveled upstream from the Gila Visitors Center. The first leg of a long Gila trip was coming to a close. I regretted more than ever my rapid progress. Either Iron Creek or Ben Lilly Cave would have been a lovely place to spend an extra day or two; now that I was entering the more used fringe area of the Gila Wilderness there seemed nothing left to do but to finish out.

At one campsite, recently abandoned, an alarming amount of debris was left scattered about - tin cans and paper sacks mostly (they could have at least burned the paper). That was pretty ugly in the wilderness. Uglier still in the wilderness was what I walked into shortly thereafter.

On the other side of the stream from where I passed by, there was a feud in progress. A man and a woman were not getting along. Perhaps one should not read too much into a conversation between two strangers when you can only hear less than a minute's worth with surreptitious ears; but I am not without perceptions drawn from experience. Few of us are. The tone was abusive, cruel; this was not simply a situation of two people having gotten up on the wrong side of the sleeping bag one morning; there was some bad blood there and it sounded like it had been around a long time. In this case - such is not always the case - the man was getting the better of it. He was working her over pretty good. The woman remonstrated but the attempt was lame. That awful imbalance that afflicts so many love/hate affairs, where one quite simply cares more than the other, had her scrambling to keep up...and hold on. I would rather not have heard it. I quickened my pace.

Nearing the wilderness boundary, and I met the Forest Service: a guy and a girl, a horse apiece to ride and two mules to pack, they were headed upstream to check it all out, make sure everyone was all right and behaving themselves. I didn't know the girl but I was acquainted with Tom. He stepped down and I dropped my pack and we shook hands. The girl stayed mounted, one leg hung over the saddle horn. We exchanged pleasantries. These were nice people and the conversation was indeed pleasant for me. I mentioned a messy campsite I'd seen. I said nothing about messy domestic strife, nor did I tell them that talking to them made me feel better. Tom said they'd clean up the leftovers and he figured they'd probably find time between such chores to catch some fish. I said I guessed they would find time and suggested they had a pretty tough job what with the weather being so nice in the spring, and a horse to ride and a mule to pack and someone nice to talk to, and them get

ting paid for all this. They both smiled and could offer no rebuttal.

Just beyond the forest service boundary I came to one of the many hot springs in the area. There were some people standing around but nobody was getting wet. I stuck my hand in the water and found out why - it would scald a nail. On a cold winter's night it would be about right.

Downstream to where the West Fork came in, doubling the flow. I was out of the canyon country now. Directly I passed under the bridge just below the Visitors Center. I waved at some tourists headed to and from the Gila Cliff Dwellings, a National Monument and major local attraction. We pressed on, Rojo and I (the tourists, judging from the conversation I overheard, found him more interesting than me) passing a ranch house, a game preserve then, finally, up off the river and across the lawn to the general store.

I tied Rojo to a juniper tree outside, left my pack there, went inside and called George. He wasn't home, but his father, Jesús, said he thought he'd be back soon. I got a cup of coffee and a big dish of ice cream. There were a lot of people wandering around inside and outside by the gas pumps, many of them with cameras around their necks. I watched them. When I was done eating, and watching tourists, I called George again. He still wasn't home but Jesús offered to try and hunt him up. About the time he said this I looked out the window and saw that old plug tied to that juniper tree and then the old gentleman walked in. I told Jesús to never mind, I'd just found a ride.

Of course this nice old boy was more than happy to return a favor; he wasn't going my way but his partner was. "I'll arrange it," he said.

SIERRA DEL GILA

I wasn't over thirty miles from home as we crossed over the East Fork Bridge, perhaps a mile below the general store. There was a good flow coming in out of the Black Range; the confluence of three streams now made a river. I'd be back in a day or two with a canoe, improved fishing tackle, other accoutrements for a long float, and a second passenger. Behind me in the bed of the truck Rojo sat animated, his long ears sailing in the breeze. Looking downstream to where the current once more entered wilderness, I saw where the Gila River made a sharp bend around a rock wall, revealing very little of what lay ahead.

"I think I could turn and live with animals, they are so
placid and self-contained...
They do not sweat and whine about their condition,
They do not lie awake in the dark and weep for their sins...
Not one is respectable or unhappy over the whole earth. "
    ~ Walt Whitman

PART II   WHITEWATER GILA

    I hadn't been close to a canoe or held a paddle in my
hands for many years. The first thing I did was misjudge the
current and was nearly swept into the pilings under the East
Fork Bridge. Recovering in time ("steady all") I waved my paddle at Thayne (he had taken me out) as he stood tall and be-
mused under the bridge; no turning back now, I was rounding
the bend, floating the Gila, headed for Arizona with a hound-
dog and a tomcat.

    The first thing that damn cat did was go over the side.
I had him collared and leashed with a light line and he didn't
get far. At the end of his rope he panicked, attempting to swim
straight up, then made a rapid cat-paddle retreat for the boat. I

77

back-paddled into the current and he climbed aboard. Wet, unhappy, he looked just like the miserable creature I thought him
to be.

I had the front two-thirds of the boat tarped down. At
the send off I had put Rojo on the bottom of the boat, just in
front of where I sat on the rear seat. From there he wanted to
climb into my lap. This afflicted my paddling. And it put too
much weight in the rear; the bow set up in the air waving in the
breeze, one reason I almost sank the ship under the bridge. After the cat climbed in I put ashore and got the dog up onto the
front seat. Twice before we were once more afloat he hopped
off. When he tried it a third time, I rapped him on the end of
the nose with the paddle. This allowed us to get back on the
water. But then he started to tightrope back over the load,
wanting once more to sit in my lap. I tapped him on the nose a
couple more times. He went back to his perch and sat down.
Soon, like the tomcat and I, he had come to accept that a portion of each day was to be spent in a thirteen foot canoe and he
began to take an active interest in his surroundings passing by.

It was warm but not hot. You couldn't find a cloud.
The water was blue or green or something in between depending on the way the light was and in the deep, cool shade of the
overhanging bluffs it looked almost black. No longer crystal
clear as it had been up above, there was a lot more of it and it
was carrying some of the Sierra del Gila downstream. I
watched my paddle as I dipped it into the flow. The tip disappeared about the time the shaft met the waterline.

Not that I was doing much paddling. The Gila's descent
is rapid. A stroke or a pry here and there for purpose of direction is generally all that's necessary and you still make time.

With the hound in the front seat we balanced fore and aft and the canoe handled well.

We rode down through some very modest rapids, then approached more significant whitewater that made a sharp bend in the middle and boiled up off a rock wall sloping away before dying a natural death in the long stretch of slack water below. Again, I hadn't done any of this in a long time. Approaching the first substantial whitewater I had a sinking feeling - augmented by a second emotion that put my heart up in my throat - that I had no idea what to do! There was a strong temptation to toss the paddle, jump, and swim for shore. In time - just in time - I forced myself to pick a route and went for it. My paddle work was not instinctive as it should be (as it must be when things really get wild) but a logical voice was working ("paddle hard left side, pry right," etc.) and presently we shot by a bad rock, bent sharply around to the left to make the curve, just nudged that rock wall as we boiled up, then shot down into the regular flow slick as you please. Skilled or lucky, it beat the hell out of walking with a pack on your back.

Coming out of the rapids, I noticed a nice looking canoe paddle drifted up against the bank. Someone had not fared as well here as I. I pulled in just below and beached the canoe. Rojo hopped out and I unleashed the cat. I picked up that paddle (now I had three). My own paddles were also fiberglass but I considered the one I found a better make and it was half a foot longer. And per chance I had stopped where scenically spaced sycamores decorated my side of the river, an impressive mountain slope clad in pines lifted up on the opposite side, and out of a fissure of rock somewhere up there a spring was sending a half gallon a minute down over a cliff into the main flow. Time for lunch.

This was more like it. With room now to carry what I liked, I was able to cut off slices of cheese and place them on crackers with those good, smelly little fish from cans. I parceled out pieces of all this to the crew. For dessert I had a real orange - no more dehydrated fruit. I licked the oil and the juice off my fingers, wiped what was left on my levis. I was back in the woods.

~ ~ ~ ~ ~ ~

Scrambling up the steep slope ascending to the hills above the sycamore grove, Rojo showed remarkable agility. He got to the top before I did though he lacked hands with which to grab and pull. Even up there our view was limited by higher hills and peaks surrounding. Looking downstream I did get the sense of the roundabout way the Gila River was steadily taking itself through the mountains into a lower altitude. And if I wasn't mistaken I saw a black and white cat way down below, sunning himself on the tarp covering a small, red canoe.

Back at the bankside I rigged up a good 5 1/2 foot lightweight spinning outfit and tossed a small gold lure here and there. In time I focused my efforts on the rock wall on the other side where a big boulder and some smaller ones lay just off the main current. In a river like the Gila where you know there are bass you have to anticipate bass when you see "structure" (a useful term from the jargon of bass-mania) like that. Creatures pursued are of course famous for confounding the patterns that fishermen, hunters and wildlife biologists set up for them, but in this case the pattern held form. I hooked a fish there on the first throw. From its struggle, which was all of lively and dogged, I figured it was a Smallmouth Bass. I let him show his stuff - a real circus on a light whippy rod - and he raced

WHITEWATER GILA

81

the line up and down the Gila. Five minutes later he lay in the shallows and I was right.

Damn cat! That's my fish! I put the 15-inch smallmouth on a stringer where a cat couldn't get it and pushed off. I had been told that the Gila between the East Fork and Mogollón Creek, (about a 40 mile run) was an endless series of rapids, many of them Class I (easy) and Class II (exciting) but a number of them ranging up into Class III (about all you can handle in an open canoe and you'd better know what you're doing!). My informants proved correct. I was not yet into any Class III rapids but already I was encountering whitewater requiring attention every few hundred yards. So far none of it was all that difficult. At least I didn't think so. But a couple of miles below the sycamore grove I saw a yellow canoe pulled off into the trees well away from the river. I checked it out. There was no camp set up and the canoe was largely empty. It had been abandoned. Evidently a couple of river runners had had a wreck and had committed the unforgiving sin of having lost their paddles. Quite possibly, I now had one of them.

By midafternoon I was ready to quit for the day. Quit while I was ahead. There were any number of places to camp that would have done fine, but I held out for the place that looked just right. I pulled the canoe up onto a firm, grassy beach. Up the low bank were some Ponderosa Pine and oak, a couple of Alligator Junipers and sycamores. Under the bigger of the junipers folks had left a big rock fireplace with seating logs pulled in around it where travelers could find comfort, warmth, and camaraderie. I packed the cooler, the duffel and sleeping bag up the bank and set it all down underneath the big juniper.

My first day on the water had not amounted to much of a workout but crouching in a canoe had left me feeling rather cramped. Also, I'd been wide awake all night at home, anticipating. I believe in the concept of *siesta* which at one time Mexicans had down pat. In rural and small town Mexico to this day, shops, laborers and work generally quit from about two till about four each afternoon. Then things humm again during the evening hours. In the larger cities, Mexicans have begun to take on the American Way and they work all day. I think they had it right the old way. And here I was in New Mexico, which used to be old Mexico, and I wasn't one hundred miles from the border. I lay on my back in the warm sun, used my canvas fishing hat for an eye shade, and took a *siesta*.

When I woke up maybe an hour later Rojo was standing nearby but looking around I didn't see the cat. With any luck, I thought, he's answered the Call of the Wild, is roaming the Gila country, and is long gone. But when I walked down to the river to get my fishing pole he appeared from out of nowhere and he followed me downstream as I tossed a lure into the flow. I didn't do any good with it so I went back to the boat and cut off a piece of ripe beef liver and I rigged up for catfish. A good rig for catfish includes ripe beef liver (it stays on a hook better than chicken liver) a sharp hook and a teardrop sinker with a brass eye which lays on the line above the leader and swivel. The weight allows you to toss the bait out to where you want it and takes it to the bottom where it belongs ("How do you fish for these catfish?" I asked the old cowboy years ago on my first attempt at cats along the Nueces River. "Put it on the bottom and leave her lay," he said. Wherever you find them that remains as good a way as any). On the bottom the bait wavers in the water a foot or so from the sinker. When the catfish takes

83

the bait he can run with it; the line runs out through the eye of the sinker and the catfish doesn't feel the artificial weight. He's fooled, and when he stops his run to take the bait down you nail him.

That's the way to do it and that's the way I did it, but again I didn't do any good. I quit with the sun going down, took a few pictures of the scenery, then rolled out six or eight hooks on the trotline, baited it with beef liver and pieces of cheese, tied one end to a bush and the other end to a rock and tossed the rock out into the Gila just below the last rapids.

For supper I fixed bacon and fried bass filets and a slice of heavy-duty whole wheat bread and butter. You roll the bacon and hot bass up in a slice of buttered bread and after the butter melts and the bass cools a little you eat it and it seems like you could never want anything else in this world. Afterwards I fixed the inevitable cup of coffee and treated it in the most marvelous manner. I had brought along a small jug of genuine New York State maple syrup that my mother had sent me. It was intended on this trip for french toast but a good dollop in black coffee turned the traditional drink into a special dessert. I don't like white sugar in coffee but dark brown sugar is good at times and this maple syrup concoction ought to be taken up by the finer restaurants. I offered the tomcat some canned cat food, but he was much too involved with raw bass guts and the fish's head. Rojo got the cat food, and kibble and grease.

I padded one of those fireside logs with my lined denim jacket, and lay back against it. After I finished my special coffee I loaded my lip with a big ol' ugly pinch. Upon need, I expectorated a brown stream at the flames. I've never been much good at this; besides making the fire hiss I dribbled on my chin.

84

I wiped it on my sleeve. From my position of contentment I could reach a stack of wood without getting up and so kept the fire cheery. I considered that I ought to go check the trotline but at the moment I had no desire to move nearly that far. It's rough in the wilderness all right, a task for the great and the rugged only; few are tough enough to chance it and succeed!

It was pretty late by the time I got on my feet to prepare for the bag. I took the opportunity to run the line. I shined the flashlight along the length of the cord while standing at streamside taking a leak, hoping for the irregular tugs and jerking that would indicate fish. Not yet.

There was no sign or threat of rain so I climbed into the bedroll without a tent. This was best - under the stars with a half moon rising. I was nearly asleep when an awful squalling, hissing and thrashing about brought me full awake. Reaching for the flashlight, I shined it at the noise and there over by a rock ledge twenty feet from camp that damn tomcat had a big Wood Rat pretty well whipped. Cat-like, and thoroughly perverse, he would enjoy this as long as he could and I watched as he repeatedly dropped the frightened, fleeing, dying rat and pounced upon it again and again. I always try to kill quickly anything I hunt and feel badly when I fail to do so but I'm not a cat. What I saw was shocking. But I must admit my own (possibly perverse) sense of Darwinian survival of the fittest was caught up with the sight of that cat's innately nasty nature in the raw. Eventually, he condescended to kill and eat that rat. I turned off the light and went back to sleep. Sometime during the night he came over and climbed carefully athwart my hips, curling up for sleep in his usual place. He must have; that's where I found him in the morning. Damn cat!

By this time a reader is probably curious, and perhaps not a little uncritical, regarding my relationship with a pet cat. A full sized-hound is an unusual companion for a wilderness canoe trip - though such a thing is not without precedent - but a cat! "If you don't like that cat" - I hear you ask - "what are you doing with him?" "After all" - you add - "that cat didn't ask to be hauled off on a 150 mile canoe trip." Well, I'd say he did.

~ ~ ~ ~ ~ ~

At 7,000 feet in the foothills of the Pinos Altos Range the "ghost town" of Pinos Altos overlooks Silver City and maintains a Post Office, a small population of interesting people, and the Buckhorn Saloon. Among other things, the steaks and the *chili con queso* are superb in the Buckhorn dining room and afterwards you can sit around the fire in the old saloon and listen to some pretty good pickers.

I frequent the Buckhorn Saloon; I am known there. In the dead of winter I began to notice on my weekly visits a black and white adolescent tomcat hanging around the door. When I'd walk in he'd try to scoot between my legs into the dining room to get out of the cold. This was not allowed and on my way out he'd be there just outside the door, cuffing at my pants leg, and sometimes he'd follow me to the pickup. One evening I spoke of this cat to another regular, a Pinos Altos resident and sometime Buckhorn employee.

"That's the Buckhorn Cat," she said. "He's a damned nuisance."

I said, "He wants somebody to take him home."

"He sure does. When I walk down the hill to the house he weaves in and out of my legs, trying to get me to pick him up."

"Why don't you?"

"I don't like cats."

"Me either," I said.

But I like mice even less and that winter my seamy little adobe suffered an invasion. I trapped a few and after a bad catch they'd squeak and flop around the kitchen floor dragging the trap and I'd have to get up in the middle of the night to complete the kill and gingerly release the distasteful carcass into the commode. When you use poison the little beggars are apt to crawl off to unfortunate places - like the oven - to die, and from there they come back in the most fetid manner to haunt you. And still I had lots of mice.

Coming out of the Buckhorn late one snowy night that cat sprang from a crouch, landed on my thigh and set his claws. "Damn cat!" I peeled him off my levis and tossed him into the cab of the truck.

It took him less than a week to slaughter *all* the mice. In the mornings I'd find their tails and little splotches of blood and fur on the kitchen floor. Mice droppings became a thing of the past. But with the mice gone and his killer instincts frustrated the cat sought other sources for his blood sport. He took to hiding behind doors and jumping out on my feet as I'd walk past. Especially in the mornings when I was barefoot on my way to the shower. An errant hand, dangling over the arm of a chair, would get cuffed. In no case did he understand how to retract his claws. And in the bedroom I have a dresser that used to stand by the foot of the double bed. It looms above the bed and an athletic cat can easily land up top in a hop and if it's late at night and you're asleep you have no idea he's crouched above you, a killer sphinx, awaiting the movement of suitable game. Even a heavy sleeper will from time to time twitch a foot, knee, a thumb maybe. That's all it took; he'd pounce, sinking his claws deep into the surrogate quarry. He got my knee late one night, I woke up angry, caught him up aside the head and sent him across the room on the fly. He hit the wall hard, landed on his feet, rolled up the skin of his back a couple of times and, twitching his tail, strutted off into the other room on his own time.

And it will happen on occasion that someone else will want to go home with me. One night - so help us - he launched a deliberate attack, with intent to maim, on the exposed, expansive and writhing haunch of a "beast of two backs." Female superior (lucky for me!). I shan't detail the outcome of that encounter other than to say she was not happy and afterwards I moved the dresser.

Clearly, a wilderness venture was the perfect outlet for a tomcat's nefarious instincts. He asked for it all right!

~ ~ ~ ~ ~ ~

I have never trapped (we won't count mice) but I believe I understand the lure of trapping. It's the sense of anticipation, wondering what you've got that morning. I understand it because I've used trotlines (fish trapping?) over the years and after the cat was rousted from his bed I was eagerly out of the bag and I hustled down to the river. At first I thought I'd struck out for there was no life to the line; but there was some extra weight and pulling it in I had a ten pound Channel Cat on the last hook. He had taken one of the cheese baits and in his twisting struggle through the night had wound himself up in ten feet of line. The struggle was over by morning. On a middle hook another catfish, probably even larger, had unraveled the braiding of the line and bent the hook in making his escape.

My catch was still breathing, barely, and I placed him in a little pool off the river where he survived for a time but never revived. He was over two feet long, heavy bodied, an old male fish who had lost his spots and turned black and big-headed for the spring spawn.

I tried fishing then with rod and bait, wanting very much to catch such a fish where I could feel him grab, pull and run in the water. I quit when I felt the sun getting hot, having caught nothing.

Catfish are the best eating freshwater fish. I included a portion of this catfish in the breakfast meal, the snow white flesh delicately flavorful. I gave the head to the cat, the cooked leavings to the dog, and in short order had the gear and the crew loaded in the canoe.

It was maybe half a mile to the first rapids - an unusually long stretch of pleasant water - and I could not help thinking I had made an auspicious start. The canoe paddle was already beginning to feel like it belonged in my hands. I had caught a nice Smallmouth Bass and a big catfish. The hound had settled into canoeing and even the cat seemed to be enjoying himself; if he didn't like canoeing per se he was happily in the wilderness where he belonged and no doubt looking forward with relish to his next Wood Rat. Canoeing the Gila was a ride of joy and the warnings of those who had attempted the river before me and had ended up walking out, I was now ready to put down as the rambling excuses that result from incompetence. I was feeling like the Whitewater King and even the discovery of another paddle and a long abandoned rubber raft below the first rapids did not change my mind. Before the day was through the Gila's whitewater did.

~ ~ ~ ~ ~ ~

WHITEWATER GILA

The yen for whitewater nearly matches the yen for backpacking and draws in large measure from the same group of outdoor enthusiasts. Skiing is also popular with the same people, especially cross-country skiing. More so than the hunting/fishing crowd, these folks are urban in background, lifestyle and orientation. They read *Outside, Canoe, Backpacker* rather than *Field & Stream, Outdoor Life* or *Fur-Fish-Game.* It amazes me that so many people run so many rivers and never fish. The "bible" of the modern canoeist would have to be *The Complete Wilderness Paddler* by Davidson and Rugge. It is indicative of the split between the two groups that the two authors had so little experience and interest in fishing that they felt obliged to call upon a third party to write the short fishing section in the book. There is no inclination here to be critical (it's an informative book and there's nothing inherently noble about fishing; it's good if you like it and that's about all) it's just that the split exists and it strikes me as peculiar because I like it all.

There's something about going down the river, whitewater or slack, floating in any kind of craft. I floated for a year as a deck hand on the Erie Canal in New York State. There was no whitewater and the boats (crane boats, tugboats and dredges) were like a floating house and industry in one and they weighed hundreds of tons. But there was the same unhurried feeling of traveling on water and each evening you were someplace new and could drop your line in the water while waiting for the cook to fix supper. We caught catfish, walleyes and bass mostly, and I can recall tossing the catfish back, not realizing in my northern ignorance that they were the best eating of the bunch. In the evenings after dark we'd find the honky-tonks in places like Weedsport and Watkins Glen. The boatmen were noted for getting into mischief of one kind or another - sometimes they even provoked it - and after one long stay on Seneca Lake I knew more about the night life of Watkins Glen than is healthy for a nice guy like me.

It was a dangerous job. I realize that now. No doubt they've since gotten out rules about wearing hard hats and life preservers (aka - personal flotation device - PFD). They may have had those rules then but I don't recall ever hearing about them and we never gave it a thought. Decking on a crane boat you've got something big and heavy hanging over your head most of the time. You're forever hopping back and forth over the water from boat to shore to the scow in tow alongside. In the spring we'd haul out the immense trees that clogged the waterways after high water and we'd cut down the ones that were leaning into the canal, obstructing navigation. Because I was a teenager and the most agile and foolish of the deck hands, I got the job of climbing out to the end of the boom with a big, clumsy, old-timey sort of chainsaw. I'd swing down onto the tree and cut it off at the nub. It was a balancing act start to finish and after the tree was in the water I'd hop off the stump onto the trunk, hook on the tongs, then catch hold of the boom with one hand, the saw still in the other, swing up, then tightrope back to the deck. The craneman, up in the wheel house with his brakes and levers, had the safest job, but one day he climbed down to help us reset the ropes on the scow. The tree hanging overhead came loose from the tongs, came down on the craneman and, with him underneath, rolled into the Seneca River. We fished him out but his back was ruined, the last I heard, forever. On that job I never suffered anything worse than a cut finger or a hangover but in retrospect it was a more dangerous river than any with whitewater that I've taken on.

Over the years there have been river trips by canoe and motorboat (mostly in Canada) and rubber raft (down the Pecos in West Texas). No kayaks; you couldn't pay me to ensconce myself into something you can't get out of in a hurry.

There was a cold rainy journey down the Mégiscane River in northern Quebec with my cousin, Hodie Soule. Soule is 6'2", real skinny, and absolutely deadpan in times of stress. This behavioral trait stood us in good stead as the cold and rain gradually, day by day, took the fun out of the week-long trip. We ran some wild ones, lined down through a few we couldn't run, and had a couple of long portages around some really big, bad water. I dislike any portage. In our better moments we stayed warm by the fire and caught walleyes and northerns, casting bright, flashy lures right from camp; we had plenty to eat. Meanwhile, the black flies ate us up during the day and the mosquitos, in spite of the cold, got us at night.

Periodically, Soule would tell a funny story, none of which bears repeating here. Not because they were raunchy. They were merely odd reminiscences from Soule's not very adventuresome life. But Soule has a way of telling them. You had to be there.

That last day we ate Fig Newtons for breakfast and made a big push for the lodge, the final obstacle being twenty miles of *Lac Fallón*. A driving wind and rain had the lake in whitecaps but we had to cross it sometime and about halfway down the lake we angled into the wind for the other side. I was in the bow and every wave slopped a bowlful of water into my lap. Our canoe was wooden, an eighteen footer, a classic model. It got us there; we reached the beach not long before we ran out of freeboard. I got out and began to run up and down the beach, both in celebration of life and to regain warmth. Soule turned his back to the wind and leaned back over the load, lit a cigar, calmly tucking his face and the weed under his stetson. And he told another funny story. I will always envy that kind of aplomb.

We reached the lodge not long before dark, suppered on fried ham and beans, and I got the old woodstove cherry red. I took the top bunk, a few inches from the ceiling, and along about midnight the temperature up there was pushing 120 degrees. Drenched in sweat, I climbed down and closed the damper to keep from burning the place up but I can't say the excessive heat bothered me much. Since then my river trips have been on water featuring lots of sun, warm days, an absence of black flies and a scarcity of mosquitos. Like the Gila.

Most folks who run the Gila use rubber rafts or kayaks; they can take a lot rougher water than a canoe. I much prefer a canoe and I reviewed makes and models carefully before making my selection. The main criteria was money. Neither book publishers nor periodicals showed any interest in financing a Gila canoe trip with a dog and a cat. Nor was money or matériel forthcoming from manufacturers of outdoor products or from the sort of people who provide grants for books. I don't blame them. I would be reluctant myself to provide money to someone who was intending to use it to have a swell time.

The Coleman canoe was the least expensive on the market. I picked up my thirteen footer in Albuquerque for $312. Cheap at the price. Hard-core river runners will observe that the Coleman canoe is not a state-of-the-art product. True. But it tracks well, handles not badly, and it's tough as a boot. My canoe has two seats and weighs sixty-two pounds. Except for calm conditions on small lakes and mild rivers it must be considered a one man boat. It will also suffice for one man and a dog and a cat.

~ ~ ~ ~ ~ ~

Even before rounding the bend I could tell there was a big sycamore down in the water. I assumed I'd get around it somehow so I didn't pull in to scout the route. Of course when you can't see around a bend you have no business assuming anything. I didn't get around it. There was no way. I back-paddled hard to limit the force of the collision but I still hit the trunk hard enough to bounce the dog off the front seat into the stream. It wasn't a rapids right there, just the Gila's regular current, or I could have gone over and under and been in lots of trouble. Rojo swam ashore. I got out on the tree and led the canoe back around the stump, picked up the dog, and away we went. Nobody needed to be there to tell me I'd made a mistake, not with the paddle but in judgement.

We ran a few more, going along good. The cat had showed no signs, since his first attempt, at jumping ship. I got to feeling sorry for the little guy, leashed up like he was, and I unclipped the lead.

From the first - and no matter how calm the current - I had to be alert all the time because Rojo was rather like packing a sixty pound bowling ball in the front seat. He was unceasingly fascinated by the Great Blue Herons that frequented the shoreline; their stilted walk always set him to whining and prancing in place, putting the entirety on a tightrope of sorts. Whenever he'd put his weight on one gunwhale or another I'd roll my own weight in the stern to compensate. It had come to seem a natural enough way to travel but, still, I had to be alert, and when we came to the first really heavy whitewater I put him ashore, shot through, then picked him up down below. He was glad for the run.

We came to this nasty, twisty, narrow stretch - not whitewater but fast and deep with a bunch of brush and branches hanging over the channel. It was pretty wild there for a little bit. I worked the paddle hard to make it through and somewhere along in there a branch grabbed my hat and dropped it into the river. When I got into the regular current down below I put in at a sand beach, got out real quick and climbed up on a rock. Pretty soon here comes my hat, floating just under the surface; I ran down the beach, waded out and picked it up. It wasn't till I got back to the boat that I realized the cat was gone.

At first I thought he'd hopped out after I'd put ashore but I looked and couldn't find him anywhere around. I had no recollection of him going over the side - had no idea whether he'd jumped out or had been taken out like my hat - but somewhere up in that fast water I'd lost him. I worked the shoreline upstream, searching among the big cottonwoods, and I called out a bunch of times: "Come back, Cat...Goddammit!" But he didn't show. I looked downstream too, but he didn't show there either. I walked back to the canoe again. I didn't know what to do.

Drowned? Not likely. I knew he could swim. Like an otter. One day weeks before I'd taken him up to Bear Canyon Lake for testing. After paddling out into the lake I set him over the side, then raced him to the shore. Cats can swim awfully fast, probably because they can't wait to get out. He fairly planed a wake - he could damn near walk on water - and he got there before I did. It wasn't likely he'd drown in the Gila where it wasn't twenty yards across. He wasn't dead, but he sure was

gone, and I'll confess my concern and sense of loss was tinc-
tured by a certain ambivalence, a creeping, cryptic exaltation.
Ours was a relationship that had never entirely worked. There
was an inherent personality clash that rather balanced the restrained affection we felt for one another; if he had chosen
freedom and hunting in the Sierra del Gila over canoeing with
me, I couldn't blame him; perhaps we were both better off. He
was certainly capable of taking care of himself in the wilderness
and if he got lonesome, in time he'd make his way to a ranch
downstream. Or drop onto some unsuspecting rafters. But I
would give him more time. I took a pinch of *Beech-Nut*, got out
my spinning rod, and started to fish.

Rojo saw him first. He whined and wagged his tail and
was looking downstream and here comes that cat, walking up
the bank on the far side, wet, besotted (they sure look scrawny
soaked down like that) and mad enough to spit. He must have
had quite a ride. I swam over, picked him up, and with a long
arm in a long arc, gave a heave. He landed on his feet on the
sand beach and immediately sat and began licking himself dry.
Rojo ran tight circles and pranced all around him. That did
make me feel pretty bad. Rojo's feelings about that cat are not
ambivalent at all, and what kind of a man would leave a dog's
favored friend alone in the wilds?

With everyone back together I took the time to make a
cheese sandwich for lunch. I fished for a while and had what
looked to be a rainbow on but I lost him. I loaded everybody up,
leashed the cat, and shoved off.

Little by little the Gila was turning into a whitewater
river. Approaching a rapids I'd stand in the boat, take a quick
look and make a decision. Sometimes it was a short straight
run and I'd pick a route and shoot on through. Often a blind

corner accompanied the roar of whitewater and I'd have to stop, walk downstream and scout the run. Occasionally, there'd be a long stretch of whitewater and I'd have to stop and look it over even though there were no blind corners to contend with. Where possible, I'd let Rojo run the bank while I ran the wilder rapids. It wasn't always possible; in places he could only run so far before canyon walls left him bluffed up. I didn't want him swimming any rapids in an attempt to follow so wherever it looked like he might get bluffed up ashore I had to keep him in the boat and let him ride on through. Of course I could always get out and line down with all aboard. That's slow, tedious, arduous work. I enjoy that about as much as I enjoy a portage. I didn't want to submit to doing any of that if I didn't have to. With a flow of less than one thousand cubic feet per second (CFS) none of these rapids were all that awesome - nothing like what I'd seen in Quebec - but blind corners, narrow canyons, rocks and boulders sticking up all over, right angle turns and trees across the river made it plenty treacherous and, like I said, it was getting worse all the time.

At one point, with the dog ashore, I paddled through this short stretch of fast water and Rojo and I ended up on opposite sides of the river. It wasn't a stone's throw across and I whistled. He jumped in and started across. He swam well until he got right in the channel where the current was still pretty strong (stronger than it looked) and it started to take him away. He turned around, started back, and began to paddle straight up and down, making splashes with his front paws, which is how a dog swims when he gets panicky. I started across, swimming, to help him. He made the shore before I got there but he'd gotten water in his nose and I could tell it scared him. Scared me too. I took him downstream where the current had eased off, talked to the boy, and we swam across together. We shoved off again, everyone still safe and sound, but no matter how you sliced it, I'd made another mistake.

My next mistake had more serious consequences. I stood up in the boat and looked down a straight run of whitewater, maybe fifty yards at most, no big rocks that I could see but some big standing waves (haystacks) right at the end. I'd come upon this all of a sudden. There was just time enough to pull into the left bank and unload the dog; I could pick him up down below. I chose to run it, as is. Those big standing waves picked the bow up into the air to where, briefly, I couldn't see a thing ahead of the boat. Rojo and the cat were still in place as we came down in a shower of river water; it was ankle deep in the boat as we shot on through. The current eddied out quickly down below into a manageable flow as the river made a right angle turn to the left up against a rock wall. We were setting awfully low in the water. I wanted to get to shore wherever I could. I pried the bow around with a hard backpaddle on the left side, then tried to paddle on by that rock wall by pulling hard on the right. This took too long (with only one paddler you can't pry around and pull through a turn at the same time) and our momentum took us up against the bluff. We didn't hit very hard - just a tap - but it was enough; the dog ("Rojo you son-of-a-bitch!") lost his balance, stepped onto the left gunwhale, tipping the gunwhale into the current, broadside; the boat filled like a glass and over we went.

I was kneeling to shoot these rapids, my feet braced under the seat, and after we went over I had a devil of a time, hanging upside down under water, getting my feet loose. When I did the current took me up against the rock wall. I got back to the surface by springing off the bottom...grabbed for air...and

there was Rojo climbing out on the left bank, and there was the canoe, headed for Arizona with a good lead, bottom up, with a cat tied up inside.

I knew I could catch the boat before it got down into the next rapids. I didn't know if I could catch it in time to keep a cat from drowning. I was not wearing a PFD; I'd been kneeling on it. Not too bright, except in this case it left me a faster swimmer.

I don't know how long it took me to catch the canoe but I remember thinking as I did: if that cat's still alive he's got gills! I rolled the canoe over out in the channel. It lay there swamped, just under the surface, and a tomcat appeared from under the tarp, broke for air, and climbed up onto the load. He sneezed a couple of times as I was swimming the outfit ashore (even in times of great stress there's nothing sillier than a tom-cat sneezing) but otherwise gave no indication that he'd taken on any water.

I placed the little guy on a flat rock in the sun and ev-erywhere I moved hard, green eyes were staring me down. Can't say as I blamed him. Over on the other side Rojo was running the bank, whining and howling like a whipped dog. With the boat full of water and who knows what all lost or ru-ined, you're asking yourself about then: what kind of a sock-and-shoe outfit is this?

I swam across and retrieved the dog, made apologies to the cat. I found I'd tied the load down well. The only things I'd lost were my hat, one paddle, and the trotline, which was wrapped around a chunk of driftwood. There was nothing ru-ined, nothing wet but what would dry off. I dumped out a boat-ful of water, reset the load, and decided that I was going to try hard to be a brighter boy from here on in.

We ran down through a few sets of easy rapids and in the eddy below the second one I picked up my trotline, floating in the foam.

The first sandy spot with some sunshine left on it I put in and made camp. I draped all the wet stuff over some bushes. Everything got dry about the time the light began to fail and I started to shiver in the chill. I put on dry clothes and warmed right up. I removed tennis shoes and dried my feet with my jacket and put on dry socks and a pair of moccasins. That helped too. Still, the day had pretty well taken the sap out of me. If I had been just a little bit dumber, or a little bit unlucky, I'd have lost the dog and the cat and I'd be looking at a long empty trip down the Gila River.

I kept thinking I ought to put out the trotline. I couldn't find any enthusiasm for doing that. I didn't feel like fishing at all. As it got dark I fed the cat as much of that big catfish as he wanted. I warmed up a can of beef stew, ate very little. I left most of it on the plate for the dog. I was almost too lazy, or out of sorts, to brew a cup of coffee. Mostly, it was out of sorts...

I don't know about you, but when I get scared, I get tender. Tender about a lot of things. Feeling tender, it's easy to feel lonely. Easy for me. I'd make it down the Gila - you'd have to be even less competent than I not to make it - but Rojo and that cat, traveling as they were, might or might not make it down the Gila depending mostly on me. That's scary. Scared and more than a little lonely, a dozen miles from the nearest road, I was wondering why I'd brought them along. And I was wishing for the first time since I'd started, a week past way up high, that I was someplace else. I wanted very much to be back where I used to be...far away, long ago...with someone. Not anyone. Someone. There was this old worm in my head and it was touching a tender place. But wherever she was now it was certain she had other things on her mind. And I didn't need anyone to tell me there is no profit, no future, no satisfaction in such thinking - it's a dead-end thought - but knowing it full well doesn't make it go away. When you enter the wilderness, don't ever think you've left the world behind.

But of an evening in the springtime along the Gila River the hop toads come out on the beach and in the firelight you watch their silly, obscene hop and squat. A hound and a tomcat know about the warted backs and the nasty taste. There is no thought here to kill but following an exaggerated leap a hound has one pretty well surrounded. He noses him over onto his back whence a tomcat, on cue, bats him around unmercifully. A toad's response is to possum. This deflates sport...until they find the next hop toad. There are enough to last until well past my bedtime. Tiring finally of sport, a hound curls up on the bag between the feet of the houndman who, this time, does not object. And later in the night a tomcat, his stare softened somewhat from earlier in the day, steps softly, hopefully, to find his place of rest on the supine form. He purrs contentment; consoled. Of course, I am not so easily fooled. There is no sympathy, no pity, in a tomcat. But then that includes no self-pity either. At that moment I shall confess I did not entirely dislike that cat.

~ ~ ~ ~ ~ ~

There is a singular thrall to running whitewater: the roar of the flow coming off canyon walls; the suspended, free-ride sense of motion; speed you cannot control, and spray in your face; the power of that water that you neither need to see nor touch to feel and know with a kind of primal tension. Only by being a little bit afraid of something can you get that kind of excitement and if you don't fear whitewater while traveling alone in an open canoe in the wilderness you are very foolish indeed. It's a kick. When you're in and out of the canoe many times a day scouting rapids, lining down on occasion, wrestling and lifting a loaded boat, and worried about two friends all the while, it's also about a job.

After a long night I was up early, crouched around a quick-flame cottonwood fire. I brewed coffee straightaway and made a french toast breakfast. But I had other things on my mind. The roughest water I would face within the Gila Wilderness was coming up. I intended to be through most of it, safely, by the end of the day.

I loaded the boat carefully, tied and tarped it all down. The crew was off in the woods but showed up before I was ready to leave. They didn't want to be left behind. On the other hand they showed no interest in getting in the boat. They showed up, I think, to ask me to stay. I placed each one in the canoe.

Foreshortening events, I will say now that it wasn't half bad. A lot of work. Exciting in places. Scary even. Properly humbled the day before, I approached Gila whitewater with meticulous discretion and avoided a wreck. Rojo ran the bank where that was feasible. On several occasions when it wasn't, I loaded him up and lined down till he could find some shoreline to run along. Then as he hopped out, I'd hop in, grab the paddle and finish the run. I stayed seated on the rear seat, rather than kneel, and got awfully good at bailing out in a hurry. Twice I was surprised by trees across the flow. I'd roll out, grab the stern line, swim or wade to shore and line or carry the boat on by. If I made a real mistake with the paddle or in judgement all day it was never a mistake of consequence.

I passed Sapillo Creek before noon, about the halfway point to Turkey Creek. It's one of those perfect spots, pretty as a picture, with a parcel of green meadow on one side, a stone beach fingering into the confluence, big cottonwoods for grace and shade, and a dark, color-stained bluff nearby features a U-shaped lip from which spring water, falling in separating gouts, sparkles down over the cliff into the flow. I stopped there briefly for lunch.

By midafternoon, I had the definite feeling I had it licked. The last rapids before I quit for the day were, for the Gila, a long stretch of whitewater. There was no problem finding a stretch of shoreline for the hound's run. I walked on down, then back up, setting a route in my mind...

~ ~ ~ ~ ~ ~

The business of using a paddle to make a canoe go where you want it to in whitewater is really not very complicated. Nor is "reading" a river. The novice is sure to pick up a book on the subject and after *reading how* to paddle a canoe is confused at best, scared witless at worst, and likely convinced that those possessing the talent were surely born in the boat. Here's Davidson and Rugge on the disadvantages of using the pry (forcing the blade out away from the boat) in the bow: "The bowman prying has neither the long extension of the draw (which allows him to lean on the power face of the blade) nor the backward angle of the stern pry (which allows a low brace lean on the nonpower face)." Good grief! After reading that I was ready to toss the paddle and revert to power boats. Actually - given sufficient time to figure it out - those boys are right. Chances are they know lots more about paddling a canoe than I

do. But any chucklehead with an IQ above room temperature
will realize that the pry is not much of a stroke in the bow. All
you have to do is try it once. Which is of course the point. Try
it! Read books about canoeing to learn about canoes, to learn
about what rivers to run, to learn what to take along. As far as
learning how to paddle one of the tippy little bastards, all you
have to do is climb in, grab a paddle, and give it a go. If you
have someone else in the boat who knows more about it than
you do, so much the better; you'll learn faster. But you'll learn
in any event if you spend some time on the water; and in time
the complex will rather suddenly become obvious, and ma-
neuvering a canoe will seem no more obtuse than shifting gears,
or reining a horse around...

~ ~ ~ ~ ~ ~

I paddled out into the flow, gave the dog a whistle (he
was meandering off upstream) and went for the chute. The
river was narrow for the run - there were no eddies to pull off in
- and the water fast and deep. The only troublesome waves
were right at the end, a line of big haystacks; but there were
three bad rocks - boulders - well out of water that I would have
to avoid. I flew by the first one easy, then paddled hard on the
right side to crosscurrent in my attempt to pass the second.
You don't crosscurrent well in fast water with only one paddle
but I got most of the boat to the left of the rock and, as I approached the rock and without changing sides, pryed hard, literally bending the boat around the obstacle. Changing sides I
had maybe fifty yards to crosscurrent again, passing the last
boulder on the right. I needed it all and, again, I pryed the
stern around the rock. Both times I passed these boulders, water boiling up off the rock came in on the tomcat and me, but
not bad. I changed sides again, working the blade to bring my-

self dead parallel with the current then, paddling hard to maintain direction, I hit those big standing waves head-on with all the speed in the river. Bow-light without the dog, for a second all I could see was blue sky. The lift absolutely scrambled that cat; he had leash enough to leap onto my chest and take an excruciating hold. There wasn't a thing I could do about it but curse ("Goddamn cat!") till I'd eased into the calmer water below where I peeled him off my body and drifted towards shore to find Rojo - incredible! - already waiting on a little finger of sand. Christ what a rush!

Shortly, downstream, I put in for camp. It had been a warm day - it was still warm - and the tomcat, clearly, had had enough sun for awhile. The fringes of his ears, especially the white one, were sunburned. He went over and curled up in the shade under a bush. My campsite held a strip of a mud flat along the bank. With some slipping around, I managed to tote everything across the mud, across some small flat rocks, to a small pocket of dry sand maybe ten yards from the water. I unrolled the trot line, baited it up and put it to work. Moving upstream I cast a small spinner.

I was hoping for a native brown of size. Because there is more water in the main Gila than in any of its tributaries the potential for fish growth is greater. Even on the Gila proper the flow is more that of a stream than a river for much of the year. Still, fish of bragging size do occasionally show up. I knew for a fact that a Channel Cat weighing ten pounds was a real possibility. Browns, rainbows and Gila Trout have been taken in the twenty inch class, though the average is perhaps half that. And Smallmouth Bass up to six pounds. What I got to start with was a twelve inch rainbow, an awfully pretty fish with colors in the water like fresh paint on enamel. On the next

cast I got a Smallmouth Bass the same length, a little heavier. This brought to mind an article I'd read one time in *New Mexico Wildlife* about how it was possible along the Gila between the East Fork Bridge and Mogollón Creek to catch trout, bass and Channel Cat out of the same pool. A Channel Cat will take an artificial, more readily than most fishermen suspect. Now I wanted a Channel Cat to complete a trio and I wished I had a jig to work along the bottom of the same pool. I didn't own a jig so I stayed with the spinner and fished it slow and deep. It took awhile, and it wasn't out of the same pool, but I caught a Channel Cat. He outfought the rainbow and wasn't too far off the Smallmouth Bass. The Channel Cat, also, was about a foot long.

I cleaned three fish - leaving the trout his skin - and doused each in corn meal. Placed in hot grease, I added salt and pepper and a sliced potato. Of course, there is no accounting for taste, or the lack of same. A great fishing book (a fine book, period) is Roderick Haig-Brown's *A River Never Sleeps*. Haig-Brown's taste in words is sublime but I can only conclude something must have ailed his taste buds. "I do not fish for fish to eat," he wrote. "Having to eat fish is one of the penalties of having been out fishing..." I wonder if he ever tried Channel Cat, Channel Cat from a trout stream...cold water catfish. I did, and bass, and rainbow trout. This is what I found.

The trout was a distinctive fish, pink fleshed and richly savory. The bass tasted more like a fish than the other two. He tasted like one would expect a very good freshwater fish to taste. Better than his largemouth cousin certainly, but, on balance, a bit gamier and a niche below his neighboring trout. The Channel Cat distinguished himself by the delicacy of his flavor. The flesh was typically snow white, subtle in taste, savory in a refined way. This, in stark contrast to the ugly-headed, bottom-dwelling fish that produced it. On my tongue a niche above the trout or bass and certainly more palatable when eaten day after day.

Trout and bass-loving readers are perhaps ready to abandon the trip at this point, what with a Channel Cat out-fighting a Rainbow Trout and offering a better meal than said trout and a Smallmouth Bass. Certainly they're all three great fish. And I'll concede I said myself there is no accounting for taste.

~ ~ ~ ~ ~ ~

There was a Channel Cat on the trotline in the morning. I had some old style farm eggs along, huge, thickshelled brown ones - the yolks more orange than yellow - from the Black Range Store near home. A couple of those plus the fish made a high protein breakfast.

I looked at the map before casting adrift. I couldn't be sure where I was but I figured I was no more than ten miles from Turkey Creek and any serious whitewater ended there. I think the crew could sense my improved optimism; they were less reluctant to climb aboard. At the first rapids, about a half mile below camp, I got out to scout a blind bend in the river. It wasn't much of a shot - I could run it with the crew aboard - but upon return to the boat I realized I didn't have my fishing rod. I knew immediately where it was. It was back at camp, leaning against a bush, right by where the canoe had left a keel mark in the mud. I'd left it by the canoe the night before so I'd be *sure* not to forget it in the morning!

Now when I was a kid, I was always forgetting my lunch. The brown paper sack my mother would place on the end of the kitchen table, right by the side door where I'd leave the

110

house for school, and at least once a week I'd waltz on by it and head for school empty-handed and without a care in the world. Along about eleven o'clock in the morning I'd start thinking about lunch and would begin to care. Then I'd remember. Invariably she'd show up, just in time, with my lunch. Years later an acquaintance of mine who had an advanced degree in psychology told me I did that to "punish" my parents. "Really!" he added. Doubtless, he would tell me I forgot my fishing pole to "punish" myself. The fact is, I was born drifty, and when the fog descends I can forget anything (my teeth if they weren't for real); after doing the dishes, I have placed the dish soap in the refrigerator. If you don't think that isn't hard to find the next day! I walked back up the banks of the Gila River and retrieved my fishing rod in full knowledge that maturity is no cure for a vacuous mind!

And there was something else I missed that day, too. A preview of government river maps prior to the trip had informed me of some remnant cliff houses, homes built and for some centuries used by the strange and wonderful Mimbres, native peoples who inhabited the Mimbres, Gila and San Francisco River drainages until their mysterious disappearance about eight centuries ago. Several hours below camp, in the midst of rapid maneuverings with canoe and paddle and dog and cat, I happened to glance to the north side of the river and saw some of these remnant houses, cliff dwellings, built into the escarpment and caves above the stream. I did not stop to look at them more closely. I knew from reliable reports that they were not as intricate or impressive as the other Mimbres dwellings at the easily accessible Gila Cliff Dwellings National Monument, which I had already seen; nor would they offer any remnant cultural treasures that I might view, beyond the structures themselves, for numerous wilderness travelers had been there before. Like I said, they are on the government maps. But I began to wish after I'd gone by that I had stopped; just to stand where they had stood of a spring morning, in front of a home built into and of their native rock, to contemplate how they might have passed their days and nights herein. For these had been a strange and wonderful people...

~ ~ ~ ~ ~ ~

They had come into these valleys as tattered bands just ages ago. They were a-foot, the entirety of the forced simplicity of their lives contained in the packs on their backs. And they had, most likely, come up from the south, off the harsh deserts of what we know as Mexico, and finding slender runs of clear perennial water coming off the mountains to the north, they settled into the valleys along the various streams where they had water and threads of level land for crops and yet could reach either the deserts or the mountains in a day's hunt. It must have seemed a glory of a find. For here between mountain and desert was a measure of land without great cold and yet relieved of great heat. Four gentle seasons invigorated by mile-high elevation, healthy breezes, and a bracing arid climate, where nonetheless water flowed for every need. They prospered in ways beyond any previous imagination. Each generation was gradually more numerous than the last, until their villages dotted the prime lands along the available streams. And each generation was better fed, housed, and clothed. In time only campfire narratives, spoken by the Old Ones and passed down from the Ancients, could remind them of the hard scrabble in a harsher land and time. Geological time would hardly mark their passing. By our time they lived a thousand years. And near the end, and end they could hardly

see coming, a modicum of primitive leisure (and the primitives, it seems, had a good deal more leisure than ourselves) and a verdant land and life yielded a generation or two of dreamers, the artists of their time. With a written language they would have left a great literature. But they could only scratch on chosen walls of native rock, and with home-made paints mark on their pots and bowls of fired soil, and there they made an art both crude and timeless, at once the sublime and the ridiculous; the mundane, and the pyramids of perception. Art of power and sadness, and death and fun; of satire and lust; of love and birth and the creatures with whom they shared the chain of life. With their art they would reach everything, from the raunch of pornography to the mysterious of the cosmos. And then, in another generation or two, they were gone. Many died. Those who lived gradually dispersed. The vegas and stream courses were left empty of humankind. Only featureless trails led away...to where? Among the artists, priests, and the Old Ones there must have some who understood what had gone wrong. But it was too late; change couldn't help them now and not even the spirits could save them. With a written language they would have left a great story for us to read. But they were artists who could only scratch on native rock and mark on fired soil with natural paints. Perhaps some of the answers lie there...

And indeed, despite the pillage and plunder of bulldozing pothunters, a number of Mimbres sites have been carefully excavated and studied, and works of art recovered and studied, and much has been learned. We have learned to discredit two myths concerning the decline of the Mimbres; that their disappearance was caused by drouth, or the victories of rival tribes. While a severe drouth did engulf southwest New

Mexico for several decades in the late twelfth century, the Mimbres were already in severe decline before the drouth hit; the lack of rain merely exacerbated their problems and accelerated their demise. And the Mimbres were long gone centuries before the marauding Apaches came into the region. Recent studies indicate a more mundane yet more plausible reason for the disappearance of a people - they overpopulated their range. It is estimated that at the height of their culture there were in excess of 5,000 Mimbres living in the Mimbres Valley alone, with proportional population growth along other rivers and streams. They killed off the game and used up the wood and timber within their range of practical use. Intensive irrigation agriculture, without rest, rotation, or sustainable cropping, eventually burnt out and spoilt the soil. They overpopulated their range, and were killed off or driven out by their very success. Some of the stress and desperation of this decline is visible in some of the art they left behind, wherein intertribal strife depicts an increasingly desperate people.

The surroundings of the remnant Mimbres life I passed in my canoe looked much as they must have looked to the people who lived there one thousand years ago. Little has changed, for this is wilderness and no one is allowed to live here now. Ironically, on private lands in the nearby Mimbres Valley where I live, population growth of we moderns is now rampant, the numbers once again approaching 5,000 souls, only now the inhabitants are high-tech consumers. The ground water table declines, and pollution is showing up in the numerous private wells, each adjacent to the equally numerous septic tanks. A culture and ambience based on agriculture and the rural life is being replaced by tract homes, trailer parks, and, as a thousand years ago, unregulated growth. And so, even as we lament the passing of the Mimbres, and marvel at the artistry they left behind, their lessons of harmony and disharmony with the natural world pass us by, largely unnoticed, as when I failed to stop and pay my respects from a passing canoe...

~ ~ ~ ~ ~ ~

We were getting good at this...without a major mishap, the pickup trucks and fishermen came into view at midafternoon about a half mile below Turkey Creek, the first people we'd seen in four days. On the beach opposite the road-head a guy got up from his folding chair and handed me a schooner of beer as we landed. The entire outfit seemed to amuse him but especially the cat. He said that he and his buddy had attempted the same run a few weeks earlier in a raft, had wrecked the raft and ended up walking out. He felt like I was real lucky and definitely crazy to have come through with a dog and a cat. Maybe so. I don't know if he was an actual cop but his cap said, "El Paso Police Department." Nice guy anyway.

In the last stretch of canyon country, between Turkey Creek and Mogollón Creek, the rapids are not severe. Here, I saw the last of the Ponderosa. It was along in here also that the Hooker Dam proposal had its focus. The idea was to manufacture a blockage of cement for the purpose of flood control and to create a lake which would back up a good twenty miles into the Gila Wilderness. The project was abandoned, due in part to the objections of conservationists, in part to the costs and because the science of geology opined that the structure might not hold. The idea for a major dam on the free-running Gila in New Mexico was moved downstream, to the Middle Box, where it promises to simmer in contention for some time.

A stay at Mogollón Creek, where I caught no fish and could see the light of a big bonfire and hear the frolic of other folks down the beach. And a most pleasant float the next day - mellow water, big cottonwoods and sycamores framing farm- land and pastured beef and horses. The Gila is used for irriga- tion along in here but it is not despoiled. We passed the village of Gila, then under the Highway 180 bridge, a landmark of sorts, where some days earlier George and I had driven over the water on our way to the trailhead at 9,000 feet. Soon we passed under another bridge and within a mile pulled into a good campsite, not far off the dirt, river road but still well hidden in the trees. I was needing a few things, particularly a hat for my bleached head, and this was a reasonable walk from Cliff.

Cliff, New Mexico 88028, is your quintessential honky- tonk village. It was in such communities that, long ago, the phrase "down home" originated. Among other things that are scarce, one finds few pretensions in Cliff. New Mexico, less de- veloped than its neighboring states of Arizona, Colorado and Texas, holds a surfeit of such towns. My own village along the Mimbres qualifies, the major difference being there's more of a Spanish influence. Either place, it's still the general store. When that goes, replaced by a Circle K, 7-11 or, what we used to call in Texas, an "ice station," you know you're starting to lose it.

As befits your quintessential honky-tonk village, Cliff has your quintessential honky-tonk: the Cow Palace. The dance hall at The Cow Palace, adjacent to the bar, is literally barn sized. There are several full sized dance floors, staircased so you can always see the band and, somehow, they draw some the best known names of Nashville, Tennessee to this remote corner of New Mexico. They (we) come out of the hills on those Saturday nights, from Grant, Catron, Hidalgo and Luna Coun- ties, and from across the nearby Arizona line. The place jumps.

117

There was no dance and but a modest crowd yet a traveler, of course, stops in at The Cow Palace before returning to the river, lured by a neon sign, the sounds of the jukebox, and the wilds of civilization. I ordered an enormous heat-'em-up pizza and the first of several bottles of Rocky Mountain Gold. After the better part of a week with my life to myself, I welcomed the change. But I had no desire to mingle. I had my table and my pizza and my beer, and I was content to watch folks...

Over at the bar, an attractive, blonde-headed young woman with a large fanny was seated on a bar stool, largely encircled by the left arm of a tall cowboy sporting a black stetson that would provide plenty of shade and a huge, blazing silver belt buckle. He also was wearing spurs. At a table nearby, a somewhat older couple sat with more distance between them than the table required. He was watching the attractive, blonde-headed young woman with the large fanny. Her gaze wandered, but wherever it went it evidenced displeasure. Nobody needed to tell me that the couple at the bar were single, and the couple at the table had been married a long time. And, a bit presumptuous perhaps, I surmised the following: large fanny, who smiled and laughed at all the right times, nonetheless wasn't going to go for it; tall and spurred had hopes but he knew they were slim; disgruntled, she'd been through this so many times she long since quit asking what went wrong; wandering eye was envious. Like so many married people, he saw "singles," of either sex, as being in a constant state of tumescence. Such tumescence, and its resolution, was something he could only imagine. I figured I knew how he felt. From a variety of experience on both sides of the fence, I figured I knew how each of them felt. If he had asked me, I would have told him that were he to conjure up half as much imagination in reference to the woman at his table (who, except for the sour look on her face, was a match for looks with the blonde) he'd be pleasantly surprised with the results. But likely I'm not the best one to tell him. I'm single myself.

~ ~ ~ ~ ~ ~

It's a "lifestyle," as they say. Sometimes I think it's the semantics involved that wear most thin with me. Single people aren't new, but it seems the lifestyle is. As best I can recall, most bars have always held a preponderance of people who are not married; married people usually have other things to do. Now we have "singles bars" and "relationships" and a "singles scene." There is even a magazine by that name, based in Albuquerque, within the pages of which contributors try, too hard at times, to convince us they prefer living that way. I don't claim to prefer living that way, but after a certain number of evenings alone in the company of a typewriter, or a book, or a hound sleeping in front of the woodstove, the walls begin to close in. It's time to get out amongst 'em. Singles bars are the logical place.

My brother calls them "fern bars." Being a resident of urban America he's not familiar with the honky-tonk variety. Viewed from his more urbane lifestyle he describes them as follows: "Lots of plants, growing in the corners and hanging from the beams, and butcher-block tables, often peanut shells scattered over the floor, and the waitress tells you her name before taking your order - 'Hi, I'm Janis. The special for the evening is the steak sandwich, with Lowenbrau on tap at half price till nine.'" Thank you, Janis.

They haven't got any places like that where I live, but in Albuquerque they do. A young woman of my acquaintance did not describe her visit to one of them with much enthusiasm. "A meat market," she said. "Don't bother!" On the other hand, this guy I know described the same place favorably. He called it a "can't miss" situation. "Bingo," he said. Bingo?

On a trip to Albuquerque to outfit for a long river trip a canoeist delayed the long drive home expressly to see what this heady stuff was all about. I went, of course, to the very place I was told I ought to (or ought not to) go. The parking lot, the size of a football field, was full. It was full inside too, but I hung around and got a table. While waiting for my order to be filled I witnessed women with incredible roving eyes wearing tailored levis tucked into knee-high boots. The men, too, wore designer jeans and if anything were more precisely coiffed than the women. The food was good, the beer over-priced, and afterwards I got in amongst 'em, eventually finding myself at a table with two guys, two women, none of whom it appeared were as yet paired off. The brunette was of a perfectly vapid countenance and it was not a lie. But the blonde was sharp as a tack.

"What do you do out there in the boonies?"

"I do the best I can."

A flashing smile. "I mean, what do you do for a living?"

"I'm a writer."

That smile again. "That sounds like something you'd hear a guy tell a girl in a singles bar."

"Well, here we are."

She liked that. When she found out I really was a writer, albeit a struggling one, she liked it even better. We struck a harmonious if somewhat illusory chord that lasted...gosh!...a whole night! Bingo!

I haven't been back. No one needs to tell me I'm out of my element in a place where the men wear designer jeans.

There are many evenings I feel quite out of my element in any bar. But when a none too successful writer is at the end of his rope, there are evenings when nothing is so bad as staying home. And so there are those Saturday nights in high country honky-tonks in Catron County, where some of the boys wear their spurs to the dance; or out on the eastern plains, in Roswell, where I've found more of an urban cowboy scene; or a certain place in Silver City which is something of both. Because of the music and dancing it's a lot less grim than at a fern bar, the pairing off less contrived and less predatory. On those nights when it's a good band it can be a lot of fun. Waltz, Two-step, or Cotton-eyed Joe, I like to hear a fiddle myself. In New Mexico a country band will often play a Mexican *cumbia* as well. During the slow dances, when you can literally get a good feel of one another, you get a pretty good idea how things are going. And late in the evening when the band's on break - so you can hear well enough to talk - you can mention a very modest adobe, and a cheery woodstove, and you can tell about the creek that runs right by the house.

"Oh that sounds nice! I'd like to see your place!"

No time like the present. It's a bit of a drive and it's suddenly real quiet and you wonder if on the way that which has begun is going to be lost. You can pick up a sixpack on the road to refresh all illusions if you're really worried.

Home, and a short walk along the creek in the moonlight, just for effect, before we hustle in and stoke up the stove. Alligator Juniper pops and crackles and piñon is a natural incense. We stand by the stove and pour two *Southern Comforts* on the rocks. The stove roars and warms the room; a peach mash liquor warms from the inside out and, not without a certain empathy and rapport, you toast a stranger you can barely see - as lonely doubtless, with similar hopes and about as much chance of finding other than temporary solace in the liaison rapidly approaching. A peach mash liquor mellows away the last remnants of inhibition; a fantasy begun on the dance floor of a honky-tonk can now come true. Without signal the moment arrives. We go down like a house of cards...

...Meanwhile, back at The Cow Palace, an attractive blonde-headed young woman with a large fanny gets down off a bar stool. She has a way of tossing her long hair around, leaving a splendid disarray parted about the shoulders and scattered over blue eyes, and she smiles, disingenuously, at a cowboy; but as she turns to leave her face clouds over. Large fanny, most desirable, takes her own discontent on out the door alone. Tall and spurred stands by himself now, staring at, and sometimes nursing, a bottle, and he has nothing to say, at all. A somewhat older couple leaves soon afterwards. They leave together; that is, at the same time. Tonight at The Cow Palace it seems like nobody wins.

Nor can a traveler stay long. He has two friends back on the river, leashed unhappily, if patiently, to a slim cottonwood. It's not far. But there's a long way to go.

~ ~ ~ ~ ~ ~

There was a diversion dam a few miles below camp. It wasn't much of a job to get the outfit around it. Next to the pool that formed behind the dam a pumping station was pumping water out of the river up over a hill to sixty acre Bill Evans Lake. Standing by the canoe just below the dam I looked at this pumping station and considered from memory the rather mundane little lake it sent water to. I wondered who Bill Evans was, and if he would have approved. In northern Arizona they dammed up Glen Canyon along the Colorado and in a very pre-

122

sumptuous bit of public relations named the resultant lake "Powell," after Major John, the Colorado's first great river runner. Not even The Major could have stopped the dam, but I'll bet the farm he'd have disavowed the name they gave the lake.

Bill Evans Lake and the pumping station and most of the water rights along this portion of the Gila are the property of the Phelps-Dodge Mining/Engineering Corporation. The lake's primary purpose is to furnish water for the processing of copper at Tyrone, south of Silver City. In a pleasant bit of public relations, the corporation works with the Game & Fish Department, the lake is stocked, and public fishing is provided. This diversion dam is a relatively innocuous intrusion on the free-running Gila. I'm not above fishing at Bill Evans Lake (some big catfish lurk therein). If a lake must be made out of the Gila River in New Mexico, an off-stream reservoir is the way to do it.

Our river had become more silty since we passed Mogollón Creek. It was a pleasant sight when we came to Mangas Creek, maybe a mile below the dam. It was clear as a bell, though it lacked the flow to clear up the river any. I knew its source, Mangas Springs, a few miles up the draw; I'd ridden around up there with local rancher Dusty Hunt. In the distance, about twenty very impressive Mammoth Jacks (Big Burros!) in a permanent pasture created an interesting pastoral scene. Rojo and I walked up there and stood by the barbed wire along the road. Every goofy looking *burro grande* in the pasture (and they were all goofy looking) came over to greet us. Crossed with the right horse, you'd get a mule-and-a-half!

Then we walked along the road to where the creek ran over and we followed it back down to the river. We were both stopping every little while to drink the spring water, which was a lot cleaner and cooler than the Gila's. I'd been drinking the river water *au natural* all the way and figured to keep on drinking it. I felt fine (if you can drink the Nueces River water unalloyed through an entire summer and never suffer you can digest the lower Gila). Nonetheless, Mangas Creek was much the better stuff.

Back at the river everyone retreated to some shade. My two friends napped. I stretched out underneath my new hat but I didn't sleep. I got to thinking...the road sign nearby on Highway 180 is curiously misspelled *Mangus* Springs. Mangus is not a word in any language; *Mangas* is the Spanish word for sleeve. Really, they ought to know better, for Mangas Coloradas (Red Sleeves) was a great man.

~ ~ ~ ~ ~ ~

In 1846 General Kearney's Army of the West traveled the length of the Gila River on the way to the conquest of California, part of the American government's self-made Mexican War. Lt. William Emory was the scribe and natural historian of the party. Kit Carson was the scout. Where Mangas Creek (called Santa Lucia Creek then) meets the Gila the Army of the West met up with a friendly band of Apaches. Their leader, of whom, sadly, no photograph exists, is described in various historical accounts as standing "six-four" or "six-six" or "head and shoulders above every white man present." He is also said to have had graying, black hair hanging straight to the waist, a stalwart, athletic physique, and a looming countenance you never forgot. Mangas Coloradas possessed other larger than life characteristics, including that of statesmanship. Apache style statesmanship to be sure.

On one of his numerous raids into Mexico he carried off a Mexican girl he rather fancied more than the rest. Nothing

unusual about that; the Apache relied upon Mexican women and children, and the resultant mixed offspring, to replenish the tribe as much as they relied upon Mexican livestock to keep everyone fed. Traditionally, a newly arrived Mexican wife was subservient to whatever Apache wives a chief already had; but Mangas Coloradas established his own traditions. His Mexican wife became his favorite and when the brothers of his Apache wives objected, strongly, he killed each one in a duel, using knives. Subsequently, his Mexican wife bore him three daughters; as soon as possible he married each one off, to one Navajo chief and two Apache chiefs respectively, one of whom was Cochise. Mangas thus consolidated both his own power and Apache power generally in New Mexico and Arizona. For some twenty-five years in this part of the world he was *the man*.

The tall chief sought accommodation, initially, with the American military. To the Apache, at this time, the Mexicans were both the enemy and the provider; the Anglos could be tolerated so long as they did not interfere with Apache raiding south of the border. There is evidence that he saw the Americans as inadvertent allies during the Mexican/American War and offered to help the American cause. After defeating Mexico, however, in a war that displayed American opportunism at its worst, the U.S. sought accommodation with the vanquished party, agreeing, among other things, to help stop Apache raiding. The Americans thus ran afoul of the Apache way of life.

I will always be fascinated by the free-spirited existence of these equine buccaneers. A scenario from that time was drawn by Lt. Emory in his report:

> *Amongst them (the Apache) was a*
> *middle-aged woman, whose garrulity*

and interference in every trade was the annoyance of Major Swords, who had charge of the trading, but the amusement of the by-standers.

She had on a gauze-like dress, trimmed with the richest and most costly Brussel's lace, pillaged no doubt from some fandango-going belle of Sonora; (what the horrific fate of the Spanish girl who originally owned the dress might have been is anybody's speculation) she straddled a fine grey horse, and whenever her blanket dropped from her shoulders, her tawny form could be seen through the transparent gauze. After she had sold her mule, she was anxious to sell her horse, and careened about to show his qualities. At one time she charged full speed up a steep hill. In this, the fastenings of her dress broke, and her bare back was exposed to the crowd, who ungallantly raised a shout of laughter. Nothing daunted, she wheeled short round with surprising dexterity, and seeing the mischief done, coolly slipped the dress from her arms and tucked it between her seat and the saddle. In this state of nudity she rode through camp, from fire to fire, until at last, attaining the object of her ambition, a soldier's red flannel

*shirt, she made her adieu in that new
costume.*

A common error of modern history, often revisionist in
tone and founded on white guilt, is to picture the Apache as a
tribe of hunter/gatherers who were forced into a lifestyle of
piracy on horseback by the Spanish, and later, Anglo incursions
on their land. In *Apache Chronicle,* the historian Upton Terrell
would have us believe Apache raiding was essentially defensive
in nature. Risking an *illiberal* point of view, I would attempt a
more accurate historical perspective.

That there was a European incursion on Apache territory is a fact of history. That the Apache resisted with violence
is understandable. It is also a fact that the Apache were war-
like raiders before the Europeans ever got here. In *River of the
Sun* Ross Calvin wrote: "Back in aboriginal times, long before
the coming of the Mexican, Apaches had been accustomed to
raiding the agricultural villages of the Pimas with the cracking
of none knows how many skulls." Walter Prescott Webb wrote
in *The Great Plains:* "It seems safe to conclude that before the
coming of the Spaniards the Apaches had already established a
feud with the pueblo Indians of the Southwest. When the
Spaniards came in they found little difficulty in working among
these pueblo Indians. Soon they found themselves taking part
with the Pimas and others against the raiding Apaches; there-
fore the Apaches made no distinction between the Spaniards
and their old enemies: they raided all alike." Bourke, General
George Crook's aide-de-camp, wrote of the blood-chilling war
dances the Apache scouts put on the night before embarking on
military campaigns *against their own people.* They liked it! Of-

ten the cliche marks a certain truth; as regards the Apache, these were "wild Indians!"

The Apache were adept at stealing Spanish horses - and were eating them - before they learned how to ride them. It didn't take them long to get a leg up; by 1630 they were well mounted, the first *indios broncos* according to J. Frank Dobie. "They are on horseback from infancy," wrote Lt. Emory. What the Comanche and Kiowa were to the south plains, and to the Mexican states of Coahuila, Tamaulipas, and Zacatecas, the Apache were to the Southwest and to Chihuahua, Sonora and Durango. Interestingly, no great conflicts occurred between the tribes. The Comanche harried the Mescalero and Lipan Apaches on New Mexico's eastern plains, but they never attempted the essential Apache homeland west of the Pecos. Down in Mexico the equine raiders kept a rough boundary, with that which is north and west of the Conchos River being Apache raiding territory. Perhaps each group realized that in the other they'd met a match. Covering one hundred miles a day, riding, stealing, trailing, eating horses and mules, the effect of the Apache on northern Mexico is best described, again, by Lt. Emory:

> *Nature has done her utmost to favor
> a condition of things which has enabled
> a savage and uncivilized tribe, armed
> with bow and lance, to hold as tributary
> powers three fertile and once-flourish-
> ing states, Chihuahua, Sonora and Du-
> rango, peopled by a Christian race,
> countrymen of the immortal Cortez.
> These states were at one time flourish-*

*ing but such has been the devastation
and alarm spread by these children of
the mountains, that they are now losing
population, commerce and manufacture
at a rate which, if not soon arrested,
must leave them uninhabited.*

At one point on his Gila trip Lt. Emory crossed a trail leading north and south marked by the hoof marks of thousands upon thousands of horses, mules, sheep and cattle. With a fine turn of phrase he thus noted for all time "the great stealing road of the Apaches."

On a mission of diplomacy, Mangas Coloradas was murdered in 1863 following an unconscionable doublecross by General Joseph West. Power within the Mimbres Apache tribe evolved to Victorio. Mangas Coloradas had been his mentor. Victorio learned his lessons well; as a leader of men at war he surpassed all other Apaches, including Mangas and the overrated Geronimo. The scourge of Victorio, with old Nana at his side, in 1879 and 1880, displayed a mastery of equine guerrilla warfare unequaled in the Indian Wars.

In the end of course the Apache lost. Victorio was killed in Mexico. Geronimo, the final renegade, went to prison in Florida in 1886. However the Apache might have outfought any opposition man for man, there could be but one ineluctable result when the foe was the American Army which, following the Civil War, was deemed the most powerful in the world.

Certain individuals involved, most notably Mangas Coloradas and General Crook, rose above the killings. For both generalship and statesmanship, each earned the respect of both their followers and the opposition.

The conflict and the tragedy were unavoidable. As to the extent of it all, one must count the inability of the Apache to make an easy transition from livestock rustling to livestock husbandry. Animal husbandry, coupled with a modicum of agriculture along the perennial streams, was a talent the Apache acquired only after a forced and total defeat.

More pointedly, the extent of the tragedy can be laid squarely in the laps of those who stood above both the chiefs and the generals. The obtuseness of the higher-ups in Washington in their insistence that all the Apache tribes make their reservation at San Carlos, Arizona was responsible for a great majority of renegade behavior. The renegades came from the Sierra Madre Apaches of northern Chihuahua/Sonora, from the Chiricahuas of southeast Arizona, from the Mimbres of southwest New Mexico and the Mescaleros of southeast New Mexico. As he was persistently throttling down Apache power, General Crook insisted that each tribe ought to have its own reservation on home territory were there to be any hope that they stay put. Crook was ignored. Even General William Tecumseh Sherman, hardly an Indian lover, commented: "I do not know the reasons for the Interior Department insisting on the removal of these Indians to Arizona. They must have been very cogent to justify its cost to the settler and to the government." Indeed the reasons were not cogent. They were foolish, disastrous, cruel.

There is little new to add to the Apache story. The subject has been covered, by sympathetic historians like Terrell, and talented writers, like Calvin. We have seen the Apache painted as nefarious savage, as the height of nobility, and, more accurately, mixtures in-between.

Searching for something to say, one could claim that the conquest of *Apacheria*, however brutally done, ultimately offered the best future possible to these Southwest Indians. Today, on the San Carlos and White Mountain reservations in Arizona, and the Mescalero and Jicarilla reservations in New Mexico, the Apache hold some of the best watered and most desirable lands in the Southwest. Not that any Apache is confined to making his life on a reservation. There are many more Apaches today than when they ruled the land. Their health is better, life span much longer, their standard of living has entered a new realm. Despite shouts, complaints and arguments all around, it's getting better all the time. But, like most of us, they aren't of much account. When Mangas Coloradas and Victorio were leading the raid, they counted. For forty years they had the U.S. Cavalry strung out at a full gallop, chasing phantom warriors. They created many myths.

Today in southwest New Mexico, once the heart of *Apacheria,* there are no Indian reservations and there are very few Indians. You stand up in the sun where Mangas Creek meets the Gila and look around and there is no sign of the Apache, at all. Over along a nearby highway there is a sign - *Mangus* Springs - slightly misspelled.

~ ~ ~ ~ ~ ~

A mile or so below Mangas Creek the Gila River once more enters the Gila National Forest, flows within its boundaries for about twelve miles through the Burro Mountains, before emerging onto private lands about five miles above the community of Red Rock. The last five miles of river within the forest is a narrow, rocky, lovely defile known as the Gila Middle Box Canyon. During a good spring runoff, which I was blessed with, the flow of the Gila through the Middle Box rates as Class IV whitewater; i.e., not suitable for canoes. I had planned to run it anyway. My experiences in canoeing the whitewater Gila with a dog and a cat sobered me up. I wasn't going to drown either of my friends in any human quest for adventure. Nor was I going to travel any of the Gila without Rojo, who had been with me from the beginning. At Cliff I had arranged with Randy Reiss and Dusty Hunt for shuttle service of canoe and cat, Dusty to handle the first part of the shuttle, Randy the second. They would truck the boat and the tomcat around the Burro Mountains to meet me at the Red Rock Bridge two days hence.

Randy Reiss wields a mean chainsaw and is a whitewater enthusiast who will try anything three times. He is one of the few to have attempted the Middle Box in a canoe. Randy, his companion and the canoe all made it through, albeit none was afloat and all were somewhat separated at the end.

Dusty Hunt is a nice guy who is becoming a friend. He is both articulate and very good with mules. How many of your friends, articulate or otherwise, are even passably good with mules? I thought as much. One hears much today about "livingroom ranchers." Most of their business is indoors, they don't care to ride, and they're mostly on the lookout for some wealthy developer so they can sell out for big bucks. Dusty Hunt is not a livingroom rancher. Dusty is what a rancher ought to be. He's up to date in the science of animal husbandry, has a masters degree in wildlife management, yet still appreciates the fact that ranching in the West is an experience as well as an occupation. He doesn't just *have* horses and mules; he *likes* them. And he rides them. When you ride with Dusty Hunt in the rough hills he calls "pastures," you seldom walk your mount. You travel at a long trot regardless of the terrain and you cover that terrain faster than you would ever believe possible. When you find the cattle, the race starts. Most of them are about half wild and a few of them are downright rank. As you

pursue this feral stock through the rough hills at a brush-pop-
ping gallop you realize that all that talk of ranching being archaic and uneconomic in the modern West pales before the
Western Myth, in action. To partake of this element of horse
culture and the Western Myth will always be worth the experience. This is no less true even if, like me, you're not much good
at it.

Once again with a pack on my back, Rojo and I headed
for The Box on foot.

~ ~ ~ ~ ~ ~

I was actually looking forward to walking the Gila for a
couple of days...until I got that pack mounted and started doing
it. The effort involved didn't bother me - I was toughened up by
now - but I walked along the floodplain and the Gila flowed
alongside and it seemed such an *ordinary* way to travel. Still, I
didn't have but maybe fifteen miles to cover and I knew Rojo
would enjoy it. It was sandy and quite open along much of the
river bank and he loped along, spinning about now and again on
a lizard chase. He can catch one on occasion, though what a
hound does with a captured lizard is something he hasn't as yet
figured out. Whenever he got hot he galloped over to the Gila
and jumped in.

Approaching the first of the rough hills that form the
north end of the piñon/juniper studded Burro Mountains, the
floodplain narrowed. Here, the narrow riparian course wound
through the *upper Sonoran* zone. I walked up through some
scattered cottonwoods to where the parallel river road came to
a dead end. The forest service sign there announced the Gila
River Bird Sanctuary. At one time of the year or another over
half the species of birds that live in New Mexico can be found
along this stretch of the Gila. In all, some 254 species have

been identified here, probably the finest riparian aviary remaining in the Southwest, according to the U.S. Fish & Wildlife Service. Grazing and vehicular travel have been closed out by the Gila National Forest in an attempt to restore the riparian habitat here to its original state, thus increasing the opportunities for bird life, and other fauna and flora. A noble step in the right direction considering that 90% of native riparian habitat has been destroyed in the Southwest. I read the sign, was properly impressed and thoroughly approved, and returned to the river.

Bluffed up. The Gila bent off to the right from a steep rock wall. I found a stout staff and backed up a quarter of a mile to where it was shallower. Crossing the main Gila was not the casual undertaking it had been on the Middle Fork but feeling my way along I got to the other side without having to swim. Rojo was leery of the prospects but when he realized I wasn't coming back he jumped in and swam over. A half mile below the crossing I dropped my pack under a big bunch of cottonwood and sycamore and made camp.

"Rojo my boy! Bait with beef liver, then set the trotline out along the edge of that pool yonder and wait on; when we get some action you come tell me about it!" Rojo is a tractable hound - he means well in all ways - but in some respects he's less than worthless. While Rojo watched intently, occasionally impaling himself with one of the hooks, I worked under a hot sun and got the line out. I adjourned to the shade and watched the sun ease off behind the hills - shadows moved in and settled in strips and patches along the vagaries of elevation, yellows and pinks came into the western sky and juxtaposed the shadows along the layered hills, scrub forest and green valley; and finally a fine scarlet came on in the sky so bright it looked artificial.

People who paint and photograph for a living often move to New Mexico for the mysteries and the magic of the colors offered in its natural world. Rojo, deep red hound, was there with me, seated tall and alert, but whether his limited eyes noticed the event at all I could not tell.

It certainly was not going to rain, as befit the lower elevation and the time of year. It hadn't rained since I was up on the Middle Fork and I had yet to use my tent on the main Gila. For my short backpacking interlude I hadn't even brought it along, and doubted I would from here on in; only a lightweight poncho just in case.

Nor had there been any wild winds, which are common in a southwestern spring. It had been breezy, but nothing to spin a canoe around or cause a backpacker to lean into a gale. The absence of rain and big winds, the sunshine you could always count on, a lack of mosquitos, blackflies, deer flies and other pesky critters, left a traveler skinning the top off a can of beef stew contending with few discomfiting elements. My head had been baked and bleached by the southwestern sun and there were still a few evil memories which that old worm in my head would tender now and again. Since Cliff, I had a new hat against the sun. As for that other, the colors at the end of a day lit promise for *la mañana*.

~ ~ ~ ~ ~ ~

You get attuned to things in the out-of-doors. Home, you'd have to beat on me with a long-handled broom to wake me up in the middle of the night; here on the Gila I easily awoke to the splashings of a catfish snared on a trotline. Nude under moonlight, a young body turned to an ancient task, I picked my way over stones and waded out, removing the slick spotted cat from the line and putting him on a stringer off where he wouldn't disturb the remaining baits.

In the morning there were no more fish on the trotline but I could see where I had lost a couple of baits. After fixing a cup of coffee I rigged up a bait on the spinning rod and sought catfish one hundred yards downriver. You can catch catfish, at times, in the bright sun on a warm summer's day; but laying the odds in your favor you'll always work them in the evening or at night or early in the morning before the sun gets on the water. In the middle of the day you'll seek water where a tree or something else has provided shade. The east rising sun was covering the far hills and coming on in towards camp, but it wasn't on the water yet. It didn't take me five minutes to catch a nice pound catfish to go with the one I already had. After a catfish breakfast, sweetened by an orange, I caught a couple more, in spite of the sun and just for fun. They squirmed and grunted like little piglets in my hands as I unhooked them and let them go.

By ten o'clock, I'd guess, Rojo and I were walking down the Gila, picking our crossings carefully, headed for The Box. Signs of an old mining operation and a trotline washed up along the bank were evidence of human activity, but I saw no people. A long-ago flood had placed some very large trees well out of the present channel, and had put a big boulder, incredibly, six feet off the ground, up in the crotch of a cottonwood!

For a ways, I studied tracks on the beach - small hand - like coon tracks; the wide prongs of a Heron's foot; an immense cat print...mountain lion!; the small cloven hoof of Javelina and, headed up a side canyon, the large cloven hoof of what had to be a big, buck Mule Deer. I stared up the canyon into an oak

grove; I didn't see the buck but easily imagined that he was there.

I'm no bird watcher, per se, but I like to watch birds. A family of ducks fled before us, the little ones unable to fly. I could not identify these ducks, they were new to me, and I wondered if this might be the rare Mexican Duck, known to frequent this portion of the Gila. Rojo scattered them all momentarily, then they regrouped in an eddy along the opposite shore. I wanted to get around them, lest we push them all the way to Red Rock and I did, finally, get them behind us by calling the dog and making a loop away from the river. Turkey Vultures, back for the summer, wheeled overhead and an immature Golden Eagle, still plenty big and with a white band across the tail, watched from a distant limb, eyeing us perhaps, but more intently, I think, mama duck. As usual, there were Great Blue Herons. Many other birds which I could not identify brightened the Gila's riparian garden and me. I did not like to think, as I approached The Box, that all of this might soon be under water.

The sound of whitewater announced The Box sometime before we got there and presently the Gila funnelled up into a canyon, with steep walled bluffs coming down to the water on either side, deep water in between, sometimes roaring white, in places deep green pools, haunts of the huge, predacious Flathead Catfish. In any event there was no place to walk!

I'd anticipated that. Rojo and I waded (he swam in part) down as far as we dared, got up on a big rock and looked down the canyon. At one point it looked like, if I could stand in the middle, I could touch both walls with my six foot span. There was a great roar and billow of whitewater right there; in a canoe it would eat your lunch. We worked our way back up to a side canyon and, after a considerable climb, got above the

Gila. From there, headed downstream, it was ascent and descent till we got to another side canyon where we hiked back down to the river's edge. We scrambled around rocks, cliffs and bluffs, along the water upstream and down, taking it all in (as much as we dared without falling in) to climb, finally, to a big table of rock where I could see upstream a short ways and downstream a long ways, all the way to Red Rock. I wasn't ready to head for our rendezvous just yet. Somewhere in here the Conner Dam was going in... maybe. If it did I wanted to be able to remember well the Gila Middle Box Canyon.

~ ~ ~ ~ ~ ~

The Gila is the last mainstem, free-flowing river in New Mexico. The waters of the other five streams that rate the title "river," the Rio Grande, Chama, Canadian, Pecos and San Juan, have all been dammed up, diverted, channelized and otherwise appropriated by a variety of human usage. I wouldn't say that's all bad - I like to fish Elephant Butte Lake myself and green irrigated fields are an antidote to urban blight - but when you're down to your last river, and they have plans for it, you realize it's time to draw the line. As well, one must note that the Gila itself has been worked over intensively in central Arizona - from about Safford on down - to where by the time you get to Phoenix the Gila is a river no more. The last three hundred miles of the stream, which centuries ago flowed all the way to the Colorado all year long, is a dry wash for most of the year. Put in perspective, those of us who oppose the Conner Dam, or any other new dam on the Gila, are hoping to preserve in its natural state just *one river* out of six, and merely *one fifth* of that river. On balance it would seem a modest aspiration. Proponents of the Conner Dam (among whom, I must say with respect, are some friends of mine) have said: "You conservation-

140

ists are going to have to give something up for the common good." From the point of view of conservation, there is virtually nothing left to give up. Not in the Southwest. Not where water and riparian habitat is concerned. We may lose the Gila too; we won't give it up.

Those more knowledgeable than I have written, and will continue to write, of the incredible use, over-use, and abuse of water in the West. They have pointed out, in essence, that Federal water development here is more often than not a catalyst for subsidized growth, rather than a response to real human need. These projects are not designed to meet growth or to serve growth, but rather to create it. Taxpayers nationwide pick up the tab (e. g., nearly four *billion* dollars for the Central Arizona Project); the natural world pays the consequences. Speaking candidly, a Bureau of Reclamation engineer once told me: "You know, one of these days Senators and Congressmen from places like Ohio may come to realize it doesn't make sense to fund enormous sums of the public's money to subsidize water and growth in the Southwest, so the Southwest can attract more people from Ohio!" But often Senators and Congressmen are the last to catch on.

Locally, most of the business community in the town of Silver City see cheap water (so long as someone else pays for it) and a recreation/tourism boom resulting from Conner Dam, and the local Chamber of Commerce provides the ongoing impetus for the project. Some other folks in the area, not all of them conservationists, see a dam on the Gila River as turning Silver City into something other than what it is - a laid back, friendly town of about 10,000, surprisingly diverse (elements of a mining town, ranch town, tourist town and college town with a near-equal Anglo/Hispanic mix) and so far spared the boomer

141

mentality that afflicts so many other southwestern communities. Silver City features an interesting oldtown architecture, and a small four year state university possessing a number of gifted teachers. The climate is as ideal year-round as nature could ever create while still providing a change of seasons, and the pace of life is as pleasant as the weather. Silver City is the kind of community people come *to,* to escape the very boosterism that would dam a free-flowing wilderness stream. Some more artists, writers and conservationists in the area would be nice, and a certain amount of growth is inevitable. Sad that Chambers of Commerce so seldom focus new prosperity on the quality of life a community already has rather than on quick fix schemes and unsavory growth promotions.

Beyond that, this canoeist can only conjure up a final comment in response to the basic contention, the big disclaimer, from the other camp - "You conservationists, wilderness buffs, ecologists and the like, are more concerned about land, habitat and animals, than you are about people!" I think this is largely true. It is certainly true in my case. In an affluent society like ours, where abject poverty is, with rare exceptions, a thing of the past, most of the difficulties we accrue in our lives, from penury to abortive romances, are our own foolish fault. Options exist for our recovery and revival. Yet land, habitat, the creatures of the wild, these have only such options as we allow. People rule the natural world today and everywhere you look we've made a hash of it. A rare gem like the pristine Gila only serves to balance otherwise overzealous commercial interests. In juxtaposition, a free-flowing stream may be the most civilized item within our realm. More than birds can benefit from association with a wild river.

~ ~ ~ ~ ~ ~

Overlooking The Box I knew I'd be back, often, so long as it was there. But I wanted to make the bridge at Red Rock before dark where Randy, probably with Ben Otwell in tow, would be waiting with a canoe and a tomcat.

Leaving the Burro Mountains, I was also leaving piñon and juniper woodlands. To the south and west, spaced nicely across the Red Rock Mesa, giant Yuccas stood stately on shimmering grasslands, the entirety mirage-like in my view midst the rising thermals. It was hot. The Gila was becoming a desert river.

BARRACA

DESERT GILA

DESERT GILA

"You never go down the same river twice"
~ *Heraclitus (amended)*

PART III   DESERT GILA

Let it never be said that Randy Reiss can't drink the hard stuff. Not to say hold it...but he can drink it.

By the time Rojo and I arrived on the scene Randy and Ben Otwell already had a big bonfire ablaze under the ancient cottonwood next to the bridge and they were attempting to slay a bottle filled with an obscure, dark amber liquid. The jug went round, the trotline never got set out, and the fire popped and crackled, punctuating a fractious and increasingly incoherent conversation. I faded out early only to be awakened in the middle of the night by a horrible growling and slobbering and thrashing about in the bushes. Ben too, thought it was a bear, a big, mean bear, come out of the hills fixin' to kill us all. It was Randy, contending with the bottle's revenge. The bottle won. We found the boy the next morning, comatose in the buckbrush, till a blazing desert sun swelled his fermenting head to where he

147

had to get up. Returning from the river surprisingly refurbished he said, "Wow Man!", and began telling me about their new "secret" catfish bait.

Anyone serious about fishing for catfish has a "secret," arcane concoction which in time they'll end up telling most everyone about, if in fact they don't go right ahead and put it on the market. Check the classifieds of the major outdoor magazines and see how many "secret" catfish baits are listed. These baits are all "secret" and they're all "deadly" and they're all "guaranteed" and it's a wonder there are any catfish left. Most anyone who knows Randy or Ben and has any interest in fishing already knows about their "secret" catfish bait so I might just as well tell you all.

Ivory Soap! That's right. Put a chunk of the soap that floats on a hook. The soap "milks," trailing its enticing odors downstream, drawing upstream to the source and the hook, catfish big and small. Catfish are a great game fish (lively, superb eating and they grow big, so what more do you want?) but they are not, in all honesty, the most difficult fish in the Gila or any other river to catch. Just because catfish have been caught on Ivory Soap doesn't make Ivory Soap the last word in "secret" catfish baits, but I'll say this: using Ivory Soap as bait, Ben and Randy already had two Channel Cats caught by the time me and Rojo and the tomcat were back on the water about noon that day. As long as they've got Ivory Soap, Ben Otwell and Randy Reiss will not go hungry along the Gila.

~ ~ ~ ~ ~ ~

The Gila was going down. The water level had been dropping ever so slightly since I'd put in at the East Fork Bridge but it was dropping more rapidly now. Floating, I could see where the water level, from the day before, had left a wet mark a good two inches up the bank. Within a few weeks it would no longer be navigable, even by a thirteen foot canoe, and I wondered if I was going to have to do much walking, dragging the canoe, downstream where the river would widen out. For now at least we floated steadily, and easily and pleasantly, not fifty miles from the state line.

A mile below the bridge I passed two men lounged in the shade on the south side of the river. They each had a couple of lines in the water. One of them rolled over to the edge of the high overhanging bank and lifted a homemade stringer as high as he could. He must have had a dozen fish strung up, all Channel Cats, nothing over five pounds. I wondered what their "secret" was, but merely waved my paddle, acknowledging success. I wondered too, about the big Flathead Catfish of the Gila which, so far, really were a secret.

The trees along the river were the usual cottonwoods, some sycamore and willow, and a few tamarisk (salt cedar) beginning to show; and for the most part all in scattered groves with lots of open country in between and the banks low enough that in places you could stand in the canoe and see out over the rolling hills which, due to the grass, looked like the hills of the great plains country far to the east; yet which, due to the occasional tall Soap Tree Yuccas, looked like a desert. These were the Chihuahuan desert grasslands of the Red Rock Mesa - less stark, less notable, more verdant than the "typical" Sonoran desert lands of central Arizona. Traditionally, photographers and writers of the Southwest have preferred the "classic" desert, the one with the big-limbed Saguaro cactus, the Sonoran; however, for the incredible, athletic pursuit of the jackrabbit and coyote with coursing hounds the Chihuahuan desert grasslands are far superior. For the houndman, a high speed chase across the Chihuahuan desert is the ultimate visual experience.

Midafternoon. I saw on the left bank a little grassy shelf, half a foot above the waterline, with a high bank behind it and plenty of shade. This grassy shelf wasn't more than six feet wide - just room for the canoe, a fireplace and a place to stretch out - but it had the look of a picnic spot and hell, what's the hurry? So I stopped.

The crew dispersed as soon as we made shore. Rojo I could see wandering off upstream, sniffing the mud flats and piles of debris, as I unloaded the boat. The tomcat disappeared into the grove. With my chores done, such as they were, I stretched out supine on green grass and shaded my eyes with my hat. Just before drifting off, the tomcat eased up beside my head and, peaking out from under my hat, I saw he had a big green lizard in a state of shock, its evil looking mouth gaping convulsively, its body impaled by cat teeth. I slept, knowing that each of us would finish the afternoon occupied, by choice, at our best respective employment.

I made no attempt to fish that evening, though I did set out the throw line; and, also different, I cooked up a plateful of macaroni and cheese for supper. Under the typically cloudless night the moon was beginning to fill; I would see the entire moon in a week.

I sat betwixt river and fire, in silence and solitude (my friends were with me to be sure but did not disturb my thoughts) until well past dark. This made it quite late for the days were increasingly long. I made my bed, waited for sleep. It was a long wait...

...Just when you think it's gone it's back, alive, in front of your eyes; the local memories, homegrown, self-nurturing, fresh, leering, taunting. That old worm in my head had life yet, and he was moving where it hurt. I knew I was in for a long night. That moon didn't help. A terrible diffused bulb, it lit the earth in a sensual glow, seeming so bright and I couldn't turn it out. It was a color I used to love, drawing back the curtains to let it in on the bed, providing light and a view for each of us, of the other, in the ferity of the midnight hour. It was ours then, and lovely. But now she slept under a different moon.

Drawn and tense from a lack of sleep, I noted the first signs of dawn, the faintest pink in the east, fading out, evolving ever brighter into an ugly, dog-eyed yellow. All before the orb. I rolled out in the half-light, quickly started a fire and coffee, piling on the bigger sticks, seeking flame, light and warmth against my demons. One of these limbs, size of my wrist, would not break over my knee. Exploding, I cracked it down over a bigger limb; the separation came up spinning, catching a serrated edge flush on the crease of the eyelid just below the brow, and in the gush of blood and stab of pain I could not see.

I made, I'm sure, unholy sounds, and I was all over the river bank reeling, stomping and rolling in panic. But whatever I'd done to my eye, it was over. In time I gathered myself to consider the damage. Using my good eye I found the river's edge, knelt, soaked my bandana from a back pocket in the stream and packed it against the eye. The wet pressure was cool and soothing; after several minutes the pain was largely gone and the bleeding began to plug itself. But with the rapid swelling I couldn't lift the lid to see if my eye still worked. I resoaked the bandana, rolled it into a headband and wound it around my head at an angle, catching and lifting the lid of my wounded left eye. Closing my right eye, I peered from under the cloth at the yellow in the east, now sun-bright, and saw the

151

lid of the orb, pushing up the colors. Close behind me, on either side of the fire, a hound and a tomcat sat watching me, the feline curious, the dog concerned. Each was clear in my view. Okay!

After one bad wreck in a pickup truck, after having been thrown off (and falling off) a number of horses, after years of fooling with such things as chainsaws and football, the closest I come to a debilitating injury is making kindling with my own bare hands. In our supremely modern age, where we have insulated ourselves so carefully against the vicissitudes of nature and the twists of fate, it is still possible to lose an eye. Especially if you are a damned fool. It had been a tough night, and I'd done it all by myself...

Perhaps this is a good place to put my "wilderness venture" in perspective: Older people (including that generation preceding mine) had it a lot tougher than me. By necessity, *they* were tougher. When the depression hit some fifty years ago, hard times drew folks down to a level of living those of my vintage can't even imagine. There was no unemployment insurance to soften the blow, no Social Security or Aid to Families with Dependent Children (AFDC). Things we take for granted, from antibiotics to air-conditioning; they didn't have them. Until the 1930's, a significant percentage of the American population grew up on horse-powered working farms. Life there before the machine age presented a physical challenge every day that we can now find only by a conscious effort. What rancher or farmer who knew how it was could view the current yuppie fitness craze with anything but bemusement.

As a member of the Post War Generation I watched many of my peers come pretty well unglued during the 1960's. Some of the rantings and ravings addressed serious wrongs and pointed out new directions well-taken. I was at the time largely sympathetic regarding the cause, but it was with some irony that I observed those who were born having it all lash out at their antecedents, who had worked so hard to give it to them. I make no attempt at humor when I say that I always figured my own parents were the best thing that ever happened to me. At times I think, better than I deserved.

As a physical trial, life today has had most of the bite taken out of it. Outdoor ventures that our ancestors had to face with a level eye, we consider as options. For pleasure, we ride a horse. For a variety of satisfactions, not all easily named, we train a hunting dog. We fish, hunt, travel the wilderness, raise some chickens or grow a garden to keep hold of our roots, not to stay alive. We canoe whitewater, race motorcycles, chase bears, climb rock walls, *creating* danger. Back then, they had the danger without asking.

The danger today - that danger we don't need to seek - is the old terror: the owl in the window, things that go bump in the night, the psychic cold. In that, things may be tougher than ever.

My father returned from World War II with a host of medals, various wounds on the mend and, it would seem, the worst behind him. Yet soon - much too soon in a still young life - certain psychic terrors killed a pretty tough guy. In my own time along the Gila (with far less to contend with) I nearly gave up one of my eyes because my own terrors over something I'd lost had me behaving as one on the fringe of just flat pulling the plug. Like him I've considered: for two-bits I'd call the whole thing off. How else do you kill an old worm in your head?

...Gently, I untied the bandana and peeled the cloth away from my wounded eye. There was a gout of blood scabbed over the lid and the swelling had vision narrowed down to a narrow and constant squint. But I viewed with pleasure all around me, and retrieved a fine green Channel Cat from the line. He flopped on the bank and sounded catfish grunts till I chunked his head. We had our fire, we had our breakfast, we had our river and another long spring day without a cloud. On down...

~ ~ ~ ~ ~ ~

Within an hour the first of the high, muted-red rock walls announced the beginnings of a new stretch of canyon country. The current quickened, the water turned white in places, though nothing approaching even a Class II rapids threatens a canoeist through the Gila Lower Box. Enjoying the pace, I used the paddle in stylized flourishes as the Gila wound around between the cliffs. The hound and the tomcat had been sleeping but they perched high on the tarp and, like me, took an interest in the new scene.

Everywhere the current came off at an angle against a rock wall, the change in the color of the water indicated sudden depth - the deep green pools the big cats and "big fishermen" love. I could have stopped and tried my luck at every pool but my pleasure of the day was in the kind of floating I'd antici- pated the entire trip, and, I knew wherever I stopped for the night I could find a promising pool.

And then there were the side canyons of solid rock - exotic, narrow defiles formed by centuries of flash floods, lead- ing away from the flow, each offering a unique exploration within a short hike. But the floating was too good.

It was early afternoon when the wind started to come up, strong, irritating (it took the mellow out of the float) gusty. I saw a cable stretched high over the river and heard falling wa-

154

ter. We pulled in on the south side at a sandy beach. The crew went off exploring in some cattails nearby while I walked downstream to check out the diversion dam. It would be a minor problem to portage around and from the top of the dam was a long view down river and right there below the dam the Lower Box ended.

Back at the canoe, and directly across the river, an enormous cottonwood promised shade. One hundred yards upstream a deep, dark pool promised fish. A quarter mile above the pool I had passed a wide canyon cut in the rocks, promising an interesting hike in the morning. Formulating the whole plan for the next eighteen hours with some satisfaction, the wind began to pick up, whipping my T-shirt about like it was trying to come off, and then my hat blew away. Damn hat! I chased it down. The wind gust was not a gust at all but a building funnel; I crammed my hat down on my head as I watched a whale of a dust devil come waltzing upstream, strewing cattails, a heavy cloud of sand and dirt, and winging sticks that could knock a grown man to the ground. On that finger of sand there was no place to run. I watched as the animals scurried off into the cattails. Incredibly, my hat once more started coming off my head. I grabbed it and dropped prayer-like on the beach, my back to the wind. It was an awful roar, a shroud of sand and sticks, and scary, but quick as that, and when I turned around my canoe was out in the middle of the Gila, bottom up, headed once more for Arizona.

What strength of wind would pick up that loaded canoe (on account of the wind I had pulled it well up on the beach) and take it out halfway across the river? I ran downstream, waded out and hauled it in. Tarped down like it was, everything was still aboard, except the paddle I'd been using, and I found it back on the beach. The crew came cautiously out of the weeds and we went across, making a breezy camp under that big tree.

All through the afternoon and night the wind blew a gale, a southwestern spring wind whipping up over the desert - hot, dusty, dry as a chip. I had to make the fire close in on the northeastern side of the tree to keep it from blowing away. And without much hope, I tossed out the throw line.

During the night I chanced the warnings of those who will tell you not to sleep under a cottonwood in a windstorm - the big branches can break loose and fall on a sleeper. I lay under the boughs and watched their moonlit configurations, moving, grotesque. The kind of night when you stay awake because, somehow, you don't want to miss it. Helpful, the animals curled up close around me. Then, in a shameful concession to technology, I dialed a small, transistor radio, settling finally on a good signal, skipping in from Oklahoma, held close to the ear. It was country music, of course, and I waited out the many bad songs for the few good ones. One in particular...

When such as Willie Nelson and Merle Haggard team up on a Townes van Zandt song like *Pancho & Lefty* you have music by anyone's standards. Such artistry leaves the usual, substandard barstool music (at once mundane and affected) sounding all the worse. Country music is both the best and the worst of the popular music we all listen to. Aided by a late night "DJ" whose approach was unusually eclectic, I heard before I slept not only *Pancho & Lefty* but as well *Margaritaville, Heard It In A Love Song,* and the mellow cross-over sound of *Peaceful Easy Feeling.* Awake in a tempest under a groaning cottonwood it was anything but that. Yet it was a memorable night and not a bad one.

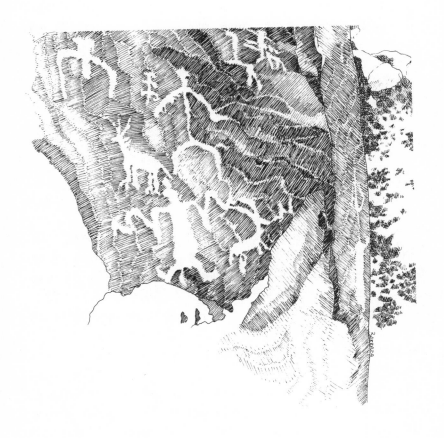

About sunup the wind abruptly went away. The rapid changes in barometric pressure that accompany winds generally botch the fishing and sure enough, the throw line was empty. I made do with bacon and eggs, leashed the cat to a bush and Rojo and I went for a walk.

We crossed the river about a quarter mile upstream, headed for the canyon I'd noted the day before. I anticipated Indian sign and (yes!) on the first of the red granite, canyon walls was an array of petroglyphs. Unlike our modern intrusions, the designs of the ancient ones were an artistry that enhanced the natural world. I'll bet they liked it here, too.

Gradually the canyon narrowed. The floor of the canyon, sediment and river sand at first, gave way to a layered bluff about six feet high that filled the canyon from wall to wall. I climbed it. On top one solid mold of off-white rock lay in waves up-canyon for a quarter of a mile. Beautiful, surreal; a canyon on the moon would look like this.

It narrowed still more, till barely shoulder width, no room for sunlight. Then the canyon floor became once again sand and gravel as the walls opened up. A series of seep springs made a trickle of water that squished under my feet. Then the canyon ended. The arroyo spread out and a grove of big cottonwoods appeared up ahead. I walked through them into the rolling hills surrounding, to the top of the highest one I could find. From there I had a fine view of the desert as it opened out to the west and south, way off towards Arizona and old Mexico. It was while I was looking straight south to Mexico that I saw faint, separated clouds of dust come fluffing up like puffs of smoke from a slow train and presently a bald faced cow and calf came into view with a horseman in full regalia in the race; riding down hard at an angle he and his sorrel horse cut them back off into the arroyo where, except for a few more puffs of dust, they all disappeared. Ride 'em cowboy!

~ ~ ~ ~ ~ ~

A high hill overlooking the desert in southwest New Mexico is as good a place as any to view the Western Myth. A significant portion of that scenario evolved within a hard day's ride of right here. Anglos, Indios, Hispanos all contributed.

The Apache, more than any single tribe, signified the Native American resistance still fondled in Old West lore. Name the great chiefs and Mangas Coloradas, Cochise, Geronimo and Victorio make every list. This was their territory. Across the Arizona line, in Tombstone, Wyatt Earp, his brothers and Doc Holiday came out winners in the Gunfight at the O K Corral. We all remember that from fact and fiction. Modern western historians continue to carp about the fact that the shooting wasn't really done at the O K Corral - rather in an alley adjacent - and they like to tell us that Wyatt and his *compadres* were just as bad a lot as the Clantons and Mclaurys. Maybeso. But it was a hell of a scrap nonetheless - only Wyatt and the Clanton who ducked and ran came out without a bullet hole. Billy the Kid rivals Jesse James and Butch Cassidy for the Famous Outlaw Award. He grew up in Silver City and began a life of violence there. Just east of Silver City, Santa Rita del Cobre was the southern-most rendezvous of the Rocky Mountain fur trade. Working out of Santa Rita, the likes of James Ohio Pattie and Jim Kirker trapped the headwaters of the Gila and San Francisco Rivers and brought the mountain man mystique to the southern Rockies. Finally, say "bandit" and the next thing you say is Pancho Villa. His horseback raid on Columbus, New Mexico was the last foreign assault on American soil. Pershing's futile pursuit of the last of the horseback outlaws, incorporating the remnants of the U.S. Cavalry and the beginnings of an air force, made him famous years before his greatness as a general in World War I. Seventy years after the fact, Willie and Merle sing Pancho's song.

The Western Myth does not want to go away. Witness the recent spate of books about the few remaining working (horseback) cowboys. We like to hold on to these things, perhaps because, as J. Frank Dobie wrote: "the climax of horse riding in America was the climax of free enterprise of the frontier kind." Horses are a remnant, an element, of the Western Myth, an element that resists change. Go to buy a horse today and they'll still tell you he's "gentle." I've yet to hear of one described as "user friendly." Thank God.

The Western Myth will not go away. It began even before the people who created it had finished their work. It is not true that Butch Cassidy and the Sundance Kid saw the first movie made about them; it is true that the first movie about the Wild Bunch played while they were still riding. Within the genre of film, the myth spawned heroes who offered inspiration to several generations of folks: Mix, Wayne, Redford. Who can say they haven't seen the films? And however oblique from historical tradition, who can say the films, the characters, didn't have an effect? Who can deny the effect on national character?

Some will comment that the Western Myth, the western hero, the West in general as depicted by Hollywood, is too hokey for serious criticism. Most folks are not like me. You can't expect them to stay up late for an old oater on T.V. featuring such as Randolph Scott or Walter Brennan, at their best. The majority of western films *are* superficial entertainment, at best. But not all of them. John Wayne features such as *Stagecoach, The Searchers, Red River*, directed by the likes of John

DESERT GILA

Ford and Howard Hawks, are among the most powerful and enduring films ever made. *Lonely are the Brave* was an excellent film made from an underrated novel (*The Brave Cowboy* by Edward Abbey). Twenty years later *The Electric Horseman* repeated the theme and caught the fancy of a new generation that wouldn't know a bridle from a cinch strap. But they liked what the film said. Indeed, examples abound - if you don't think *The Treasure of the Sierra Madre* is a good film you've been jaded by too many Space Odysseys.

One definition of myth describes legends derived from historical tradition. The Western Myth in film did not derive from made up sources or fanciful achievements. The violence, gunslinging and marksmanship of the period have been greatly overdone. The horsemanship and physical toughness of the myth makers, famous, infamous and anonymous, is as often missed by those who chronicle the frontier. Consider: Mangas Coloradas and his band, raiding deep into Sonora from their home in the Sierra del Gila, riding day and night, trailing herds of stolen livestock a thousand miles at a killing pace; Billy the Kid, who broke jail one evening, killed a man and stole a horse and, without changing mounts, covered one hundred miles to safety before he saw the morning sun; Buffalo Bill (William Cody), riding relays as a youthful pony expressman - 332 miles in twenty-four hours. All that happened. Such is the stuff of myths.

Can we name the source of the myth, find its wellspring? Can we explain its continued appeal? How come the Marlboro Man still sells? For this we look to literature.

A few years back a group of western-based writers gathered in northern New Mexico to toss the Western Myth in literature around. What made the papers was the disparaging commentary of certain of the more politically correct writers who opined that the Western Myth was unkind, inaccurate and unsympathetic in regards to certain minorities and sundry of the downtrodden. These are the sort who will deride Twain's *Huckleberry Finn* because the relationship between the white boy and the black man is not deemed sufficiently egalitarian. Criticism of this type is sometimes true but largely irrelevant. In art it is of course the medium, not the message. Or ought to be. The Western Myth in literature does not revolve around any dialectic. Its essence is not a communal spirit.

The source of the Western Myth, the wellspring, is the frontier. Real people, operating largely on their own in a big wild country, faced enormous challenges, both physical conflicts and moral dilemmas, for which there was little precedent, either for their actions or behavior. Some extraordinary characters(not all of them laudable) emerged. Also some great source material, for literature, art and film. Not all of these characters were cowboys and Indians. There were trailblazers, *voyageurs*, river runners, mountain men. The Western Myth moved West just ahead of civilization but it emanated in the east, when it was our frontier. Fenimore Cooper's *Leatherstocking Tales* were an early expression. Then came Thoreau, our first and, next to Aldo Leopold, our most elegant definer of wilderness and its value to us. Huckleberry Finn found wilderness, and solace, floating the Mississippi, civilization on either side, and when his river trip was done sought to "light out for the territory ahead of the rest," thus maintaining certain liberties he had defined for himself. As for the trans-Mississippi west, it is said that it has yet to produce a great literature. Maybeso. But there have been some very good books: *The Treasure of the*

DESERT GILA

Sierra Madre, The Call of the Wild, The Big Sky, Desert Solitaire, The Milagro Beanfield War, and a canoeing book...

...John Graves, a canoeist with a lyrical gift, traveled the Brazos River in Texas in the 1950's, just before dam building there began in earnest. In *Goodbye to a River* he preserved his journey and that river in an extended essay. Both the book, and the Brazos that was, are now part of the myth.

The essence of the Western Myth is not any communal spirit, but rather the primacy of the individual. Within the historical tradition, and the legends it produced, we find these larger-than-life characters who *made things happen to fate;* collared it, throttled it and kicked it down the road. Or at the very least they tried. Such characters remain appealing today, indeed are all the more appealing, what with our modern life and its artistic expressions beset by a surfeit of whining, self-doubting, angst-ridden heroes whose individualism partakes more of narcissism than any claim to forthright behavior.

"In wildness is the salvation of the world," wrote Henry Thoreau. Great stuff that, and also his answer to the bleeding hearts and self-doubters - "However mean your life is, meet it and live it; do not shun it and call it hard names. It is not so bad as you are."

Our frontier is long gone away. Our wilderness exists as ordained parks; like the Western Myth, as much a reminiscence as a reality. Yet we hold on to both, and rightly so.

Standing on a high hill overlooking the heartland of many a legend, a traveler beset with his own self-doubts finds the Western Myth both pertinent and up to date. He'll take it, in fact and fiction, myth and reality, the history and the art.

~ ~ ~ ~ ~ ~

Back in camp it was evident from a tomcat's demeanor that he was not happy with having been left behind, tied to a bush. He was pissed! I turned him loose. That, I figured, would improve his spirits straightaway, but as we all walked along the large sandy beach just upstream from camp he was still quite sullen, lagging behind, walking catlike and very carefully in a straight line, failing to take his usual interest in his surroundings. You would expect that he would be off stalking about, looking to kill something.

This sullen behavior on the part of a tomcat was not lost on Rojo who by nature is a bit of a tease. As the cat sat impassively on his haunches, his nose in the air, the hound began to gambol and cavort on the sand; directly he made a couple of tight circles, working up to speed, before taking a long, swift run at the cat. He broke away from his sprint at the last instant, kicking up a shower of sand, as the cat blurred the air with two particolored paws filled with extended claws. And he hissed and spat. Rojo loped away, made a big circle, and began working up to speed once more. Each time he made his run and pass he came closer to those slashing hooks. I was watching two remarkable athletes play a scary half-serious game. The last time Rojo feinted a pass, then attempted to leap up and over the cat. It was an impressive leap and quick as light but springing off his hind legs the tomcat also cleared the ground and caught the hound a good cut in the belly. Rojo yelped and by the time he landed lightly on all fours he'd decided to quit. As an athlete, I lack hand-to-eye coordination, but always felt I could lay some claim to quickness and agility. Watching those two in mock combat makes you realize just how far any human athlete has to go.

DESERT GILA

The hound and the cat wandered off into the weeds, separately. I went fishing. Soon, I'd caught a bullhead. I looked for the cat...this would cheer him up. But when the cat appeared he had better fare - a half grown cottontail, absolutely innocent, whose purpose in life, now that she was dead, was to feed a feline and revive a killer's smitten spirits. "Tomcat," I said, "You're incorrigible." But he is inured to criticism.

I loaded the canoe and paddled a quarter mile downstream to the diversion dam. There I had to unload it again. If I'd had a partner we could have simply slid the whole outfit over the dam; as it was I had to tote everything around to the shoreline below the dam and then I slid the empty boat over the top. Like I said, I dislike any portage (a canoe is made to float people down rivers, not tote around) but this wasn't a real portage and it wasn't ten minutes till we were back on the water.

The diversion dam was taking a quantity of water and putting it into the irrigation canal on the north side. Below the dam the river widened out. So for two reasons it was shallower down below the dam. There was still enough water though, and so far the channel wasn't hard to follow.

A pretty good wind came up against me. For the first time on the trip I had to kneel in the canoe and paddle hard and steadily to make time. I didn't like that at all. I was spoiled. A few miles below the dam we crossed underneath a road bridge just shy of the Mormon farming community of Virden. I was not exactly burning up with ambition this day, could see no reason to hurry, and I knew there was a good chance the wind would be gone in the morning. With my eye on some dark clouds billowing up in the west, I made camp just below the bridge.

DESERT GILA

I ate an orange, fished upstream (particularly under the bridge) and down, hoping for a big Flathead Catfish. Even a little Flathead Catfish. I didn't catch anything. I heated up a big can of *Wolf* brand chili and fed the dog (kibble) and the cat (that bullhead). Late evening the large bank of dark cloud that had been rolling around in the west came on over and for about an hour we had a pretty good rain. Underneath some young cottonwoods I fashioned a tent from the canoe tarp and I hooded up underneath there with the crew and smoked my pipe. We were all real quiet and listened to the rain and watched it fall. After the rain a splendid orange and pink sky framed by a rainbow blossomed briefly then went down with the sun. That was a picture for a man with a camera and talent. I had a camera but not much talent and whenever my interests are committed to looking at the best of things, taking pictures is the furthest thing from my mind. I brewed and drank coffee, took a leak, brushed my teeth and went to bed under my homemade tent. But it didn't rain again.

~ ~ ~ ~ ~ ~

We got an early start in the morning, it was clear, and there was very little wind and we drifted on through the trees with farms on either side. I watched a big Turkey Vulture perched on a high snag drying his six foot outstretched span in the morning sun. They'll do that. Especially after a wet night. After we'd gone by, and not because we bothered him any, he took flight - a ponderous beginning with spacious flappings in slow motion followed by an effortless rise once he hit the rising thermals over the desert. "Ugly" and "graceful" are not necessarily contradictory words; they exist in the same bird.

At certain places - where the cottonwood and willow was sparse and the bank low - I stood in the boat to get a

DESERT GILA

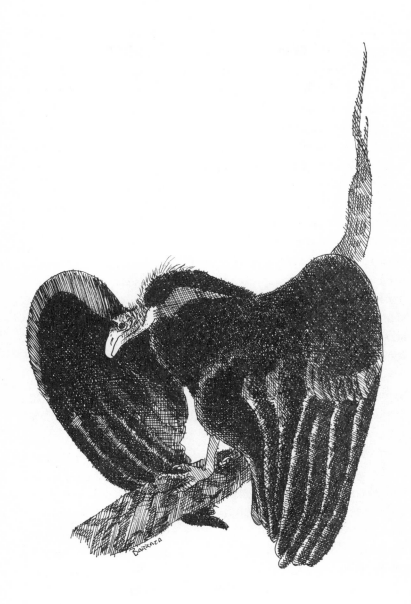

glimpse of the countryside. There were irrigated fields scattered along the river. And every little bit, small streams of water that had been diverted upstream for crops came trickling back into the Gila. I was no longer traveling a wilderness stream. But agricultural use of the water along here was not really intensive; that would come further downstream at Safford. Approaching the state line, the Gila still wound around like a river, and riparian habitat (streamside vegetation) was still lush; it had not been removed, nor had the stream been channelized in an effort to put every last acre foot of water to, as they say, "beneficial use."

Of benefit to whom? Good question. Traditionally in the western states, including New Mexico and Arizona, "beneficial use" of water means, by law, consumptive use of water. It simply isn't allowable for a person, agency or group to purchase a river water right and then leave the water purchased in the stream; the water must be diverted out of the stream and put to "beneficial use;" i.e., consumptive use by agriculture, municipalities or industry. This water law bias in favor of development leaves rivers like the Rio Grande, the Pecos and the lower Gila dry much of the year, with a consequent loss of riparian habitat, waterfowl, bass, catfish, beavers and muskrats and riverine recreation. Knowledgeable conservationists are pushing hard in the West for a change in water law and management that will allow for "instream flows" or, "instream use" of water rights. Such a change in western water management could essentially restore rivers like the Rio Grande, Pecos, and others, as natural areas, providing another sort of "beneficial use," as when in pleasure I floated the Gila one spring morning with a hound dog and a tom cat, under a stunning blue sky.

DESERT GILA

Very close to the Arizona line, within that finger of Hidalgo County New Mexico that juts up into Grant County terrain, I came to another diversion dam. This dam had less of a drop. I dispersed the crew and eased the otherwise loaded boat over the falls. No problem.

Just below the dam I directed the canoe into a little clearing on the south side of the river and put ashore. Over on the north side, directly opposite, a much larger sand beach provided access to the river via a public road. There was a pickup truck parked over there and an attractive family of four had a picnic going on the beach. The parents looked to be about my age and there was a boy maybe ten and the little girl was maybe eight years old. By indirect glances we were all spending a certain amount of time looking each other over as we went about our respective pursuits. I was seated in partial shade peeling an orange. They were cooking and eating and fishing and laughing and running around and everyone over there was obviously having a real fine time. They also were speaking a lot of Spanish (I caught commentary in both languages concerning that goofy cat), but when the father waved at me finally he said: "That's what I always wanted to do!"

I said: "Go for it!"

He laughed. "Hell, maybe next year," he said and shrugged his shoulders. I tipped my hat...

...The grass is always greener on the other side of the fence, or river. Across the stream was a man who would very much like to take three weeks off and float the Gila. Certain responsibilities made such an escape more difficult for him to accomplish than for one as unattended as myself. From where I sat, the scene across the river was so pleasant, so rich in humanity, so bucolic, it hurt. I wanted to go over there and visit but was much too shy to risk an intrusion.

One never feels so lonely as when in the company of those who are not. Looking across the Gila, the juxtaposition drew out reluctant thoughts - the years pile up, as do the abortive romances, and you begin to lose track of both, as well as the bad decisions and worse choices. It also begins to dawn on you that perhaps you are not after all a woman's perfect prize. Viewing those who have found something you never had, you wonder if, in that way, your number is ever going to come up. And it may have been my illusion, but that Spanish language made the contrast all the more vivid for me. The Hispanic population has held on to the spirit of family rather better than some other ethnic groups. Or so it seems. One is especially conscious of this in New Mexico, our most Hispanic state. About forty percent of all New Mexicans speak Spanish when they feel like it; in much of northern New Mexico and in the southwestern part of the state Hispanics are the majority. All things are still not as they should be, but in my part of the state the relationship, the mix, between Anglos and Hispanics is more congenial, less biased, less race conscious than other places. Northern New Mexico for example. Or south Texas. Do my Hispanic neighbors retain familial pleasures the rest of us are losing? It may have been simply my mood, but certainly the scenario across the Gila made me think so. Whatever, I share the Southwest with a handsome, competent race, among whom are the most beautiful women I have ever seen. One in particular. Thoughts of one in particular come easily to a canoeist seated in partial shade, peeling an orange, watching a fine family along the Gila; and above, the light floating desert clouds that arid breezes blow so easily away. Ah well!

DESERT GILA

~ ~ ~ ~ ~ ~

Shortly, down river, I crossed the boundary from the great state of New Mexico into the great state of Arizona. Although there is no sign along the Gila to mark the crossing you can nonetheless see the change. In the distance, to the west and north, multicolored Arizona mountains were scattered monoliths in the desert basin. Under a lifting sun they displayed a passing fancy of variegated light, shade, tone and tint. All bald rock - or so it looked from the Gila - while back over my shoulder, to the east and north, New Mexico's Burro Mountains were clad in piñon, juniper and pine. Much as I like New Mexico - prefer it - I must admit that for classic desert terrain, Arizona runs the lead.

Crossing the state line into Arizona the subject of state chauvinism quite naturally presents itself. Despite a supposedly declining regionalism most folks are still quick about blowing the horn for their home or adopted state. It's not hard to get us to say why we like one state, or don't like another. There is some rivalry between New Mexico and Arizona in that each regards itself as the quintessential southwestern state. I tend to avoid the argument myself; I live in New Mexico but not very far from the state boundary and I spend time each year in Arizona, fishing, hunting, goofing around; I like them both. The superiority of the Arizona desert has been remarked. Arizona has nearly three times as many people (there are more people in "greater" metropolitan Phoenix than in New Mexico) which earns it no plaudits from this canoeist. New Mexico has a more pervasive Hispanic culture; Arizona has more Indians and retirees. On the outdoor scene, Arizona's Rio Colorado rather overpowers New Mexico's Rio Grande and it is better preserved. On the other hand, New Mexico has that fine expanse

173

of short grass prairie, the Llano Estacado. Otherwise, outdoors, the two states are too much alike to conjure up much of an argument. You run the list of game animals and game fish in the two states, the ecological variety, the amount of public land, the climate, the congeniality and professionalism of the respective game and fish departments (they're both exceptionally good) and you can just about take your pick. It's a horse apiece.

So you look to Texas, New Mexico's neighbor to the east, for an argument in state one-upmanship. Lord knows Texas is chauvinistic. And Lord knows New Mexico complains. Texans overrun New Mexico's ski resorts every winter. They are very influential in business; eastern New Mexico, New Mexico east of the Pecos, is often referred to as "little Texas." The way I see it, the two states are too *dissimilar* for much of an argument. Texas boomed long ago and is still forging ahead without a backward glance. New Mexico remains relatively primitive. I lived in Texas for about ten years, remain very impressed, but with my outdoor orientation it's really no contest. There are no mountains to speak of in Texas, no wilderness, and worst of all, no public land. The big state's growth rate is enough to send any conservationist elsewhere.

You want an argument? A good honest debate? Try New Mexico versus Montana.

Acknowledging, finally, a more settled state of mind, I sought some years back to pick a state and set down some roots. I considered Montana and Idaho in the North; New Mexico and Arizona in the South. Idaho and Arizona went first. Montana for a time held a certain sway. I had been there and liked it. It's a big country, not many people, with both great plains and great mountains and awesome opportunities for outdoor recreation, and a number of very fine writers have extolled its virtues. New Mexico appealed for the same reasons, got the nod because its laws and outdoor opportunities are more congenial to the houndman (e.g. you can't hunt bear with dogs in Montana), plus I am the anomaly that prefers catfish to trout. Finally, I felt a certain subliminal appeal towards the Southwest that, at the time, I could not explain.

I picked New Mexico and haven't regretted it but more than once an enthusiast of Montana has put up a pretty good argument. Allowing for a certain compilation of discourse, the argument goes something like this:

"You like the outdoors," Montana says, "you really like to hunt and fish - why don't you move to Montana where you've got it all?"

"No place has got it all," I respond, "but New Mexico has more of what I like."

"What about Mountain Goat?" Montana says.

"Barbary Sheep," I respond.

"Sharptail Grouse."

"Gambel's Quail."

"Grayling!"

"Flathead Catfish!"

This went on for some time. Nobody could make a point for which there was not a counterpoint. Finally, leaving off specifics, he drifted into a vague realm, something he called "quality of life."

"The Big Sky country," he opined, "is just a great place to live."

That's where he made his mistake. Seeing an opening I went in for the kill.

DESERT GILA

"What do you do in Montana," I said, "when you get an aching urge for a big ol' ugly bowl of *Posole,* or a Chicken *Chimichanga* with green chile and sour cream?"

That shut him up. Montana, I'm sure, is a great place to visit.

~ ~ ~ ~ ~ ~

Pleased with the thought of having passed into a new state, I (we) floated on into an increasingly desert-like environment. On the north shore a finger of land edged out into the river and right there, not two feet from the water, was a pair of cowboy boots and a tall broadbrimmed hat of similar style. There was what looked to be a scarf tucked into one of the boots. That's all. I anticipated a swimmer but I could see a good ways upstream and down from where I was floating along and so far as I could tell there was no one around. Odd!

I levered the canoe around and put in just below these items which were rapidly activating my curiosity. I approached the evidence, tentative, wondering? Because I've hunted some I instinctively looked first for tracks. There were a lot of small flat rocks on this beach; I nonetheless expected to find a people track in the sand leading into the water. There was none. The boots, on closer examination, were brand-new, knee-high, needle-nosed and belonged (had belonged?) to a woman. Ditto the hat and the bright, expansive scarf. This was a perfect scenario for a suicide note. I looked carefully in the boots, under the hat, under rocks...nothing doing. I replaced everything as I found it and, feeling suddenly like whatever it was that was going on here I was intruding on it, shoved off.

For the next mile I was a careful observer, expecting at each bend of the river to discover the body, tightly ensconced in form-fit jeans, silky print blouse, beehive hairdo still intact, her name on the back of her belt. But if she was floating the Gila too, I didn't find her. I would have said something if I had.

The Gila began to narrow between high dirt banks. The current picked up, fast smooth water. The vegetation on either side was thick and impressive - enormous cottonwoods, close growth of willows and pink-tinted tamarisk, all leaned into a canopy over the river. The trees were wrong (there was no cypress, cabbage palm or live oak) but it nonetheless reminded one of a river float in the deep South. So I lay back in the canoe and we rolled along in the shade and every once in a while I dipped my paddle into the current to maintain direction. It was like that for several miles, right up to the highway bridge that crossed over the river adjacent to the town of Duncan.

I pulled in under the bridge, leashed the hound and the tomcat to the canoe - left them in the shade provided by the bridge - and walked the half mile it took to get uptown.

Uptown, there wasn't a whole lot - no distinguishing architecture, no monuments of historical importance. The most notable edifice was what used to be the movie house, on main street, its lower section filled with several feet of silt from a recent flood. Due to the irrigation along the Gila, this was a farm town more than a cow town. Like any other small town in the Southwest, folks waved as they drove by, perfunctorily to be sure. But at least they weren't in too much of a hurry to be friendly.

I found a cafe and ordered a hamburg steak dinner, including french fries, green beans, a glass of buttermilk, apple pie and ice cream. While waiting for delivery I adjourned to the men's room to wash up. There was a mirror over the sink and, unavoidably, for the first time in a week, I got a good look at myself (if you could call it that). A deep, ruddy complexion indicated many days under a desert sun. The left eye was swollen, discolored, the sclerid bloodshot, but recovery was evident. Otherwise the eyes were deep set and blue. The face was scruffy with a new growth of dirty blonde beard. The hands were cut, red and callused. This guy had gained weight, as happens to most scrawny people when they've been working hard and eating good. He was still lean as a snake. Summing up this bit of self-indulgence, I decided I looked like something the cat drug in. I'd never felt better.

After lunch (dinner here in rural America) I went down the street to a grocery store and picked up a few things I was short of. I put it all in a box and carried it back to camp. There I turned the crew loose, stretched out under the bridge and took a siesta...

Rojo and the tomcat were not happy that I left them once again under the bridge when I went uptown for the evening. That was a hurt look I got, from either source. But I could hardly pass up the chance to explore the night life of Duncan, Arizona. Wearing my cleanest dirty shirt, with my hat set at a new angle, I went looking for the wilds of civilization and a neon sign.

It took about an hour of walking around to see the rest of Duncan. As for neon signs, there were two bars and one steakhouse. I had a couple of beers at this one little bar set off the main drag, then adjourned to the steakhouse in anticipation of the biggest T-bone they had. Looking like the most common disreputable canoeist, there was some concern on my part that they might shoo me back out the door. But nobody batted an eye and indeed there were a couple of truckers in there who if anything looked worse than me. There's no excuse for that.

DESERT GILA

I savored my T-bone steak dinner and later, at the other bar, I got to talking to an elderly ol' boy who was working with some race horses near town. He was pretty drunk and entirely garrulous and anyway, it's pretty easy to make conversation about horses in a small southwestern town. Gradually, this bar began to fill up; six guys came in together and commenced taking turns, two by two, at the pool table. I began to notice that one of these guys was giving me the eye, and a grin - he'd evidently noticed me as a new face in Duncan and I thought: this sure is a friendly town.

The evening wore on. The pool balls popped. The juke box played the usual run of barstool music and along about midnight I was up at the jukebox making a selection of my own when I got a pool cue in the ribs. It was the same guy with the same grin but it didn't look so friendly anymore. When, a short time later, I overheard a portion of his conversation - something about a "goddamn narc!" - I began to feel like I was catching on. I began to think things might could get a little "western" here in Duncan, Arizona.

As an aside - before the rest happens - I would state firmly that I am not a narc. It is not an occupation that has ever interested me. Concerning that most commonly used controlled substance I seldom imbibe and never condemn. Concerning anything more serious than that I am blithely ignorant. I suppose I could have tried explaining that to this guy, but I was once again sitting on a bar stool talking horses and I figured if somebody in there wanted to think I was a narc that was his problem. Then his problem became my problem. He walked up behind me, took my hat off my head, put it on his head, and stepped into the men's room.

179

The classic barroom confrontation! And well done! I've got your hat, what are you going to do about it?

I slid off the bar stool and all of his buddies were grinning at me. This maneuver had not only been clever, it was well planned. The old man I was talking to, the horse trainer, seemed to sober up all of a sudden, and he said: "Did he just take your hat?"

I said: "Yes he did."

"What are you going to do?"

"I'm going to go and get it."

"Wait a minute," he said. And he stepped into the men's room.

The man who took my hat did not strike me as much of a physical specimen; I would not, if I'd been he, have attempted to take my hat. A little close quarter violence in the men's room and I'll lay a dollar to a doughnut I'd have come out of there with that hat. Whether I'd have gotten out of the honkytonk, or out of Duncan, Arizona, with my hat, or all my teeth, is very doubtful. In retrospect, one is certainly better off losing a three dollar canvas fishing hat than a row of front teeth, or the continued use of a straight nose; but you can't just let a man take your hat. Not when you're a wilderness traveler canoeing the Gila and have half a dozen beers elevating your capabilities.

It would have made a great story but - alas! - no sooner had the old gentleman stepped into the men's room than another of those pool players stepped up, accosted me, and said: "Bro, my friend thinks you're a narc."

I said: "He can think what he likes, but he can't have my hat."

"Are you a narc?"

"A narc? Hell I'm a canoeist!"

"A canoeist? Wait a minute," he said. And he stepped into the men's room.

The old man knew for a fact I had a canoe. The second interlocutor apparently believed I did. Paranoia was placated. Shortly, I got my hat back. The intercession of the reasonable had prevented a brawl I was sure to lose.

Under the bridge, I slept next to my pistol that night. Plus I had the hound; nobody was going to sneak up on me with Rojo around. I slept fine. No problems. Duncan, Arizona had lost interest in me.

~ ~ ~ ~ ~ ~

We left early the next morning. Before breakfast; indeed, *without* breakfast. I'd had enough of the wilds of civilization. Like Huck Finn, I felt safer on the river. Once on the water I parceled out odds and ends from the cooler to the dog and the cat. I drank from a half gallon of buttermilk I'd bought in town and so we had a leisurely breakfast on the float.

In many places the channel undercut the bank. I imagined huge catfish lurking under there. It's the sort of place they seek to hide in during daylight hours. Made me think of ol' Buck, the guy from the U.S. Geological Survey office whom I'd talked to on the phone before the trip, inquiring about the Gila's flow rate. Buck's pretty chatty. When you talk to Buck on the phone you get more than the flow rate. He said: "It's running seven and a half feet at the Red Rock gauge - that's less than one thousand CFS - where you goin'?" I told him where. He was enthused and we talked on for a good while; useful conversation from my point of view because Buck's an old river rat who grew up near Duncan. When we got to catfish he had quite a story:

DESERT GILA

"Me and this other guy - I was about fifteen years old then - took this big ol' flathead from out of the Gila near the state line and hung him on the cotton scales at Duncan. He weighed forty-two pounds and drew quite a crowd." That's the kind of story (and you just *know*, talking to Buck, that he wouldn't lie) that inspires the imagination of a river runner and catfish enthusiast. I imagined forty pound Flathead Catfish lurking in rivery dugouts at every turn.

Catfish that big do, in fact, live in the Gila. In true rivers, and in lakes, the Flathead Catfish may exceed one hundred pounds. Also the Blue Cat (Huck and Jim snared a six foot two hundred pound blue on the Mississippi!), present in portions of the Rio Grande and Elephant Butte Lake, but not in the Gila. One wonders how the "Big Blues" would do in the Gila. I suspect they'd do very well. More so than the Channel Cat or Flathead, the Blues require relatively clear, well oxygenated waters. They are the least adaptable catfish. The Channel Cat is the most adaptable. I've caught them in a trout stream, and in a farm pond that's little more than a mud wallow; from the Red River of the North, on the outskirts of Winnipeg, Manitoba, to the Nueces River in south Texas. Two introductions the New Mexico Game and Fish Department ought to consider: Blue Catfish in the Gila, and Snowshoe Hare in the Mogollón Mountains. That would give me fresh new sport, in summer and winter.

At night, these days, with spring advancing and the altitude dropping (the altitude at Duncan is about 3500 feet) it was barely what you'd call cool. In the daytime it was flat-ass hot (over ninety degrees, I figured, even on the water)! Rojo managed to get in the water pretty much whenever he wanted, keeping himself cool. The tomcat didn't like the heat, but he

183

didn't like the water either. *For his own good* I periodically took him by the scruff of the neck and dunked him into the Gila. Pissed him off. But he felt a lot better, in spite of himself. As for myself, concerning the heat, I'm a lot like the old desert rat (you find these individuals in various disguises scattered across remote areas of Arizona, New Mexico and West Texas) who said: "I was only too hot once in my life and I liked it!"

I have experienced the climatic extremes available in the lower forty-eight. I have lived in regions of great cold, like Lake of the Woods County, Minnesota; and hot places, like McMullen County, Texas. At forty-four below zero with a good north wind, when your hound lifts his leg to pee on a tree, the squirt freezes before your eyes right there on the bark before it can dribble to the ground. I wouldn't believe it either if I hadn't seen it myself. In Lake of the Woods County I watched the temperature stay below zero day and night for seventeen days straight. I've watched, and felt, the temperature rise above one hundred degrees each day for I don't know how many weeks in south Texas. It was humid too, and no air-conditioning on the ranch. You learned to sleep in sweat. Then when the sun came up, it got hot! I don't like one hundred degree weather but it's merely unpleasant; when it gets way below zero it's scary. Not that it kept us indoors. We caught coyotes in below zero weather. Still, that's too damn cold. That kind of cold is a big reason I left Minnesota. Compared with south Texas in summer and northern Minnesota in winter, an arid float along the Gila in Arizona at ninety-some degrees is very close to pleasant.

~ ~ ~ ~ ~ ~

You look at the map. There are so many fine-sounding names for towns and places in the Southwest - Presidio, Terlingua and Wink in West Texas; Luna, Pilar, Artesia in New

Mexico. Arizona has some good ones, too. Apache Grove is one of my favorites. I couldn't see that community from the rock canyon where I camped for the night but by the map I wasn't far from it. Another of those giant cottonwoods shaded camp there. A railroad track ran along by the river and right up against the rock wall. There wasn't anyone around.

Filled with visions of pole-bending Flathead Catfish, I camped in this short stretch of canyon because I liked the looks of the deep green pools that lay up against the rock walls. Such pools can be deceptive. They are the haunts of big catfish; however, the cats hood up in there when they're dormant, not feeding. When they get hungry they roam around, lurking about and stalking food where there's current - above a rapids, below a riffle, on the edge of a flow or in a backwash. So you look to fish the currents in the *vicinity* of deep green pools. Also, if you're seeking catfish of size you're chances are better with live bait. I'd been pretty lazy about this. Wanting a big catfish more and more I took the time to hunt a little mud flat vegetated by cattails near camp and caught three or four Leopard Frogs and put them in a can. Using just a bit of a sinker, so the bait could move almost naturally, I fished in and around the currents and backwashes and caught two Channel Cats pushing eighteen inches that each did a fine job of bending my pole and running my line up and down the Gila. But *big* catfish, of either species, weren't biting. I put one of those catfish on a stringer. I ate the other one for supper. I also had a can of stewed tomatoes. I am very fond of stewed tomatoes. And, for dessert, I satisfied a growing yen for sweets by eating a couple of cans of chocolate pudding that I'd picked up in Duncan.

A small plastic bottle of dish soap with an open/close squirt hole in the top is one of the handiest items you can have along on a canoe trip. With it you can wash your dishes, your self, your clothes, and you can shampoo your hair. Much more versatile than a bar of soap. Still plenty of light left, and still plenty warm, I tossed out the throw line, then stripped down and waded into the Gila with my handy plastic bottle of dish soap for a long overdue bath. The first couple of feet felt like bath water, deeper it was cold, and that good current washed the soap off my body and out of my hair as well as any motel shower. Refreshed (I should have done that before!) I got a change of clothes out of the duffel, put a wash and rinse on the rest and hung them on some bushes to dry. Rummaging around in the duffel I discovered an item for my reading pleasure - a copy of *Hook & Bullet* magazine that I'd forgotten I'd thrown in. Knowing I'd forget it all over again if I put it back, I set it aside for the appropriate occasion. I chunked up the fire and hung around the flames while I watched and listened for the dark...

When, on the desert, the wind quits for the day it gets very quiet indeed. Sounds that remain travel enormously in the dry air, mingle well with the muted sluice of the current, the occasional crackle of the fire or faint rustle from calming leaves; and, in the dark when you can't see well, you listen better. I could hear faint, undifferentiated sounds from the community of Apache Grove. Periodically, I could pick out a truck shifting gears along the highway. I wasn't but a mile or two from human goings on but I nonetheless felt quite secluded, undisturbed. It only takes the right place, a certain mood and a little imagination. The lower Gila River is not a wilderness but some of the feelings of wilderness can attend one camped along it if you're creative and alone with a small personal moment. Thoreau, lest we forget, ensconced himself in a semi-permanent camp on the shores of Walden Pond but a mile or two from Concord Village and within sound of both the Fitchburg Railway and Emerson's dinner bell. From there he tramped the woods, fields and farms and oared about the pond, and wrote of the outdoors, and of wilderness in particular, as no one else has. We'll fight it all the way, but our future will nonetheless witness an increasingly populated out-of-doors and a shrinking wilderness. Some of Henry's creative perspective must necessarily attend our own vision and perceived sounds if we are to enjoy those small personal moments, along the Gila or elsewhere.

Late in the spring means not only hot days but long days. I sleep late in the winter because the sun is late waking me up. Late in the spring I arise with the chickens, especially when I'm sleeping out-of-doors. I could faintly hear an Arizona rooster as I lay in the half-light just prior to rolling out of the bag. There were two Channel Cats on the trotline, neither of them as large as the one I had on the stringer from the day before, which was still alive and swimming (a trout or bass would have been dead, pale-ugly and poor eating by this time). I turned the two on the throw line loose. Then I strapped on my .22 revolver, leashed the dog, tossed a couple of pebbles at the cat to keep him from following, and went jackrabbit hunting.

I had to walk up the railway line a ways to find a draw in the rocks leading away from the river. Pretty soon it all opened up into some low, gently rolling desert kind of country featuring scattered cholla bloomed out in bright yellow, and reds, and purple. For an hour or two past sunrise it is often possible to spot a hare that's moving about and feeding, before she hoods up for the day in her form. Generally, when I hunt jackrabbits I use a hound. Rojo's grandmother, a small, lithe sylph of a hound named Cricket, who had the speed of a Greyhound and a lot more endurance, was one of the best. Rojo, athlete that he is, is still not fast enough to catch a jackrabbit. He has too much trail hound in him. On this morning, hunting with a pistol, I saw one jackrabbit moving around, feeding, but could not get close enough for a shot. Then, a sudden apparition, one bounded up almost from under my feet. Sometimes they'll stop running if you whistle at them; I whistled, but she kept up a long, leaping lope till well out of range. Then against all odds she stopped, and allowed me to walk up within twenty yards. From a crouch, my arm steadied on my knee, I squeezed one off and drilled her through both shoulders with a long rifle solid. I ran up there and stomped her head and she quit kicking.

I gutted her right away, then took her back to the Gila for the rest of the cleaning. I fried the hare, made some gravy, put it all in a saucepan, covered it up and let it simmer. Meanwhile, I fried up yesterday's catfish and fed it to the crew. You quick-fry and eat a jackrabbit like a piece of chicken and it's generally just as tough as you'd imagine. Cook one slow with plenty of gravy and they come out fine, accompanied by the rest of my stewed tomatoes.

I did the dishes. Then I picked up reading matter and adjourned to a smooth, barkless, horizontal cottonwood limb that lay about two feet off the ground. There, well seated for a certain necessity of nature, I perused an issue of *Hook & Bullet* magazine.

~ ~ ~ ~ ~ ~

There are a great many versions of *Hook & Bullet* magazine, many of them regional in orientation, or devoted to a particular facet of outdoor sport, but as most are aware there are three national, broadbased hunting/fishing magazines.

These three magazines change editors frequently and, as frequently, the editorial slant of the publication may change. Inasmuch as the better known editors and writers often make the rounds from one magazine to the other each publication can, over a period of years, end up reading like what the others used to be. Generally, and excepting a few exceptional writers and editors, the approach of most all these periodicals is pretty much straight outdoor journalism. In a way you can't blame them. The American Hunter/Fisherman apparently wants a straight shot of information and technology in the woods or on the water and I'm sure there are computerized polls to prove it. For that matter, the non-consumptive outdoor magazines, read by backpackers and fitness/health enthusiasts, are equally enthralled by equipment and technique over the aesthetics involved in the outdoor experience. Send in a piece that does not feature state-of-the-art gear or precise expertise and you are inviting a rejection slip, no matter how well you put words together. Huck Finn, I'm afraid, wouldn't qualify as an outdoorsman today, nor his creator as an outdoor writer.

My copy of *Hook & Bullet* featured an article on the presumed threat of meeting bears in the woods (a very toothy bear drooling savage saliva that fairly dripped off the page graced the cover) and the presumed effectiveness of various handgun calibers in meeting the threat. Stuff and feathers! True, you can kill a bear with a handgun, of any caliber if you hit him in the right place. And true, a grown bear could, if he put his mind to it, kill any unarmed man alive. It *has* happened. But anyone experienced in the outdoors knows that a bear is the least of your problems. Chances are *much greater* that you will suffer and/or die because you got lost, or had a heart attack, or drowned, or got shot, or walked into a wasp nest, or

had a car wreck on the highway getting to or from the woods. Or got jumped by some muggers. A handgun where bears (or muggers) are present is not a bad idea; the subject is hardly worth the annual, sometimes bi-annual, feature that some editors of *Hook & Bullet* are wont to put on the cover.

I turned the pages. A useful column about hunting dogs. A good conservation article. And feature after feature telling us where-to-go and how-to-do-it. Not bad writing. But the former (and I've written some of these myself) get to reading like Chamber of Commerce promotions; the latter smack of product advertising. Mind you, one cannot write of the out doors without putting it on paper where you went and what you did there. When the promotion becomes the focus of the piece you let the literate reader down. I looked in vain for the evocative essay, the telling tale with an outdoor theme, the writer whose slant was off-the-wall, provocative, thoughtful or creative. And I thought of *The Hunt*...

John Mitchell's book came out a few years back, a literate, balanced look at the ethics and aesthetics involved in sport hunting, produced by a major publisher and it even made a paperback edition. Here was a chance for some serious self-examination. Other than a short, *noncommittal* book review, *Hook & Bullet* all but ignored it. Ironically, there are a host of outdoor writers out there whom I know for a fact are capable of evoking serious, literate themes were there editors and publishers to turn them loose. Most all these periodicals now do fine work with photography and graphics; the same creative steps could easily be made with prose.

Is it possible that all this is sour grapes from a none-too-successful outdoor writer? Maybeso. In any event, disgusted finally over contending with, even to just myself, the ethics and aesthetics involving the outdoor media, I decided not to contend with it. My call from nature satisfied, I tore out the several pages of *Hook & Bullet* describing the terrible threat of bears in the wild and put them to good use. Feeling much better I picked up, packed up and shoved off.

~ ~ ~ ~ ~ ~

Below the short stretch of rock canyon where I had camped the Gila, as I suspected, spread out between widened banks and for the first time I ran aground. I pulled the boat over the sandbar, got back in the channel. For the next several hours, until I once more entered canyon country, I read the river, watched for the channel. Sometimes I read wrong and had to push through, poling with the paddle, or get out and walk. But it never amounted to much of a hassle.

Approaching the Highway 666 bridge I came around a bend into some fast water - no rapids, just some rapid river. Off in the shallows some big carp were rutting around, making waves and showing their fins. All carp, it seems, are big, and powerful, and watching them rut around in the spring reminds me of the several I've caught on rod and reel, and many others I've skewered with bow and arrow, and how the biggest of them, once hooked or arrowed, towed my boat around! Intrigued by big, rutting carp, I didn't see the stout dead limb hanging over the water; it caught me across the chest and swept me out of the boat slick as you please. The eviction was so subtle the canoe was not upset. I grabbed the stern line on the way out, resurfaced, pulled in the canoe, bounced off the bottom and back into the boat. No hat though. That damn hat! Regaining the paddle, I hurried downstream to a riffle, beached the canoe, hopped out and climbed a rock. Sure enough, here comes that hat, rolling along just under the surface. Well practiced at this, I ran downstream, splashed out there and got it. On down...

Under the highway bridge, then a railroad tressel, then another bridge, below which I spied a barbed wire fence. I had seen the remnants of numerous others along the way, all washed out by the spring runoff. This one was up. Using the paddle I hit the skids, rolled out into the shallows and, lifting a strand, eased the canoe on through. Rojo took the opportunity to jump over the side and do some exploring on shore. I floated on down a ways without him but when he didn't show up, pulled in on a sand bar and whistled a couple of times. No dog.

Over ashore, on the south bank, there were a couple of guys back in the trees a ways stringing fence and rigging up a corner brace. I went over there and greeted them. By the certain shy and deferential demeanor that greeted me I understood before they said anything that they were *braceros* (workers) from across the border. I am not without feeling concerning such people, or their troubled land. My sympathies and regards go out to both. I once spent some time in Mexico, and I fell in love there. She was a woman of her country. My affection for each had something to do with the way I felt about the other. On the Gila, with me conjuring up what remains of my Spanish, we had a little chat and, though they didn't know it, my memory was fondly piqued. Like everyone I'd met along the way, they were pleased to hear about what I was doing. Having strung some miles of fence myself, I commented that it wasn't the best job in the world. But they had no complaints. They hadn't seen the dog but offered to help look. We all walked back over to the river bank and about then Rojo appeared way up the river at the fence, standing in the water where we'd all gone through

DESERT GILA

the barbed wire. I whistled and he ran, swam and splashed on down. These guys got a kick out of that.

I shoved off and waved my paddle and there was lots of *buen viaje* and *que te vaya bien* and *mucho gusto* all around. Good folks!

While I was floating the Gila these guys were operating as common criminals, probably the most common criminal in this country - the illegal alien. Estimates vary, none are reliable, but certainly the "illegals" number in the millions. Most of them are from Mexico. Also while I was floating the Gila the U.S. Congress was debating legislation designed to curtail this criminal activity by beefing up the border patrol (necessary at certain border crossings), and by leveling fines and perhaps jail sentences at employers who hire these people (a police action that may cost more than it's worth).

Although I am innately skeptical of many of the cries of "discrimination!" that appear periodically on the front page, and on the screen during the six o'clock news, in this case the fears of the Hispanic community are not unfounded. Certainly in the Southwest the legal status of many newly arrived Hispanics can fall into a vague realm. Some have no "papers." Some have good "papers;" others carry phony ones. Some have (had) "papers" that may or may not have expired. Some *mojados* (literally - "wets") have been here so long they have become in effect common law citizens. In fear of hiring an "illegal," an employer might well turn away an American of Hispanic descent, one just as "legal" as myself, whose Spanish is better than his English. Such people are not uncommon. Legislators in Washington, once they are elected, are wont to *do something;* i.e. pass some laws. They often thereby create a hassle that makes the problem addressed seem minor in comparison. The legislation proposed (and likely to pass) is potentially discriminatory, is definitely anti-libertarian, and ignores the realities of the situation; i.e., the migrant from Mexico is not a refugee, but an unemployed person, the great majority of whom have no intention of living permanently in the United States. They work cheap and hard at a job nobody over here for the most part is willing to do. While here they spend money and consume, pay sales tax, liquor tax, gas tax, etc., while drawing nothing from Social Security, unemployment insurance, AFDC, medicare or food stamps. Then they go home to Mexico, hopefully with a little nest egg. It is ironic (and pertinent) that most of the opposition to such legislation comes from legislators and governors who inhabit the southwestern border states where these "illegals" are supposedly such a problem.

This has been my traditional view of the matter, but I'll concede my own bias on the issue stems from pleasant association with *braceros* who come across along remote stretches of the border and work in rural areas; i.e., farm and ranch hands. These people, it seems to me, are not numerous, are certainly unobtrusive, and serve a real need for labor. Increasingly, however, I must concede a preponderance of evidence indicating that illegal immigration from Mexico now largely occurs in or near cities, is increasing rapidly, and it may well be that much of this influx comes to stay and is permanently swelling the population of already bloated border communities, while draining local welfare systems, and the tax base, already strapped. Legal immigration, at some 800,000 per year, is already way beyond the worthy goal of population stability in America, and illegal immigration, along with the high birth rates of the poor and uneducated, of all races, that are already here, surely exacerbates the problem. It has been said that we cannot protect 2,000 miles of border from illegal immigration. But we don't need to protect 2,000 miles of border; we only need protect a few miles within and either side of the large urban areas where most of the "new" illegal immigration is taking place. At that, border control, however important, is withal a band-aid cure. The essential problem, of course, is that Mexico has overpopulated its range, which is, for the most part, a desert. Deserts were not designed by nature to hold an abundance of people; unless we wise up to that fact, on both sides of the border, we're all in trouble.

~ ~ ~ ~ ~ ~

Running water of any sort being on the order of a rare gem in the Southwest, what there is tends to be of great interest to those who would either commercialize it, conserve it, keep it inviolate, or use it for recreation. Those rare, pristine gems like the upper Gila (I was now within twenty-five miles of the end of the natural Gila) which have neither been greatly commercialized nor overused for recreation, necessarily stand out as the region's most precious treasures. With mixed emotions - not wishing to inadvertently promote either commercialization or overuse - a canoeist herein reveals another river (stream really) within the region which stands out with a similar appeal.

The San Francisco River forms in the White Mountains of Arizona and heads directly for the nearby New Mexico line. They've got it plugged up right at the border, forming a pond called Luna Lake, but a trickle of it carries on, picking up a rill or two coming off Escudilla Mountain and a few others, like Centerfire Creek, over in New Mexico before it runs through the town of Reserve. From there it streams on into the Gila

197

National Forest once again, picking up Tularosa Creek, Negrito Creek, then a good stream, Whitewater Creek (remember that?) at Glenwood, below which it turns back west towards Arizona. From there, for about 40 miles (about 20 miles on either side of the border) the "Frisco" runs through as lovely a riparian canyon as you'll find in the Southwest. Nice enough that a portion is under consideration for protection under the Wilderness Act. Needless to say, there are those who would do other things with it besides leave it alone.

The battle over the Frisco Canyon is a classic example of easy access versus wilderness style recreation. Although there is no road *per se* in the Canyon a well-equipped off-road vehicle (ORV) can, during much of the year, make a fifty mile run all the way from the Frisco Hot Springs, where the canyon begins, to Clifton, Arizona. During the 1960's ORV use in the canyon began to increase markedly. A diverse group of conservationists began to lobby the Forest Service to exclude vehicles and to consider some kind of wilderness designation for the canyon. Several ORV groups, in particular the Las Cruces Jeep Club, lobbied in kind for their right to use the canyon as a road. Through it all the Gila National Forest, managers of the region, has consistently sided with the ORV users - "Off-road vehicle use in the San Francisco River bottom is not at present presenting unacceptable resource loss," has been the standard forest service response to the conservationists right up into the 1980's.

On two occasions the Forest Service has commissioned outside researchers to inventory the ecology of the canyon, including assessments of ORV damage to riparian habitat. In 1973 Dr. John Hubbard, endangered species director, New Mexico Department of Game & Fish, and Dr. Bruce Hayward, Western New Mexico University, studied the canyon and filed a report. In 1982, Steve Carothers of the Museum of Northern Arizona did the same. Both reports noted significant damage to riparian vegetation from ORV use and, contrary to the forest service belief that high water each spring wipes out the tire tracks, demonstrated that ruts from ORV's lead to channel cutting during high water which exacerbates the erosion originally begun by the vehicles.

Hubbard in particular is adamant about the value of the Frisco Canyon as a wilderness riparian area.

"I don't know why the Forest Service remains so stubborn on this issue," Hubbard told the Albuquerque *Journal.* "The damage caused there (Frisco Canyon) by ORV's has been documented, but the Forest Service refuses to recognize their own research. This is really a crucial issue. I know of no riparian area in the Southwest that compares to the Frisco Canyon in opportunities for wilderness and solitude."

In the 1970's during RARE II (roadless area review), the Frisco Canyon became a wilderness study area (WSA); however, vehicular use was still allowed. The obvious inconsistency here - how can you study an area as a wilderness without treating it like a wilderness? - escaped the Forest Service. Now, in the 1980's, the Forest Service plans to drop the area as a WSA, thereby solidifying ORV use there for future generations. Of course confirmed wilderness lovers like me will always push for a wilderness designation, wherever we can get it. Knowing we often don't get what we want, it makes sense for conservationists in the Southwest to focus their attentions on the riparian areas. For running water, when undisturbed, provides an ecosystem, a life zone, all its own; a riparian swath of cottonwood, sycamore, Emory Oak, walnut, hackberry and dozens of other streamside plants that can nourish over the length of one stream everything from *Canadian* zone forests down through *Sonoran* desert. It is in the desert regions - as along the Frisco Canyon, or the Gila where I traveled - that the narrow winding trail of the riparian zone shows its best effect, forming a continuous, tenuous oasis that trails through an otherwise arid land and multiplies species of plants, birds, fish and mammals along its route. It is often said that the Southwest offers six life zones - *Alpine, Hudsonian, Canadian, Transition, Upper Sonoran, Lower Sonoran.* There is a seventh, a *Riparian* zone. It is the most fragile and variegated of all. It should be reserved for those willing to visit as nature intended.

~ ~ ~ ~ ~ ~

After picking up the waters of the Blue River and passing through the town of Clifton, the Frisco once again begins a circuitous route through canyonlands. Shortly, it merges with the Gila. With the Gila narrowing up once more - great rock walls again surrounding us - I approached with great anticipation the confluence of the two rivers within the Gila/Arizona Box.

~ ~ ~ ~ ~ ~

Were I to ever (and someday I might) set up a semi-permanent camp for a stay of a year or two, it would be at the confluence of the Gila and San Francisco Rivers. Either there or up above, where Sapillo Creek joins the Gila. Either location would be secluded, scenic, and largely self-sustaining for an enterprising outdoors person. Either would be classic Southwest. All within the context of a most pleasant change of seasons. When, standing in the canoe, I looked over the last little spit of land that formed the final separation between the two rivers, saw the green Frisco about to make its juncture with the more silted Gila, that's what I wanted to do...stay...for a year or two.

DESERT GILA

The campsite provided was precisely as I would have it if I were a creator of natural campsites. There was a small sandy beach on the Gila side where I beached the canoe. This little triangle of sand was backed by a one hundred foot rock wall, and fronting the Frisco was a rock ledge maybe three feet high that overlooked deep, swift water. I could set out sundry odds and ends there like I was using a shelf, and the water below looked prime for fish. It was mid-afternoon and very hot but brush and trees growing out of the base of the bluff gave us the shade we needed.

The crew promptly found the shade. I waded in knee deep, filled my hat with water and put it directly back on my head. I stood around in my little place in the sun for awhile while I dripped dry, then side-walled the bluff, making my way up the Frisco to where the bluff ended and a shoreline opened up. I meandered upstream in the rock canyon of the San Francisco River. Then I wandered on back. Besides cottonwoods and other riparian growth, there were ocotillo cactus and mesquite of the *Lower Sonoran* life zone. At the junction of the Gila and San Francisco Rivers, I thought that perhaps I was at the true heart of the Southwest. And then I saw the desert flower...

A cactus flower of the Claret group, growing incongruously out of a seam in rock and so scarlet it marked your eyes. It caught me. No domestic flower, not a tulip nor a pansy nor a greenhouse rose, can equal the tone, tint or flush of color provided by any number of flowers that grow in the desert. This can be seen to be true by any disinterested eye; it is made the more so by the fact that the desert flower blossoms amid such starkness. The brightness then, can provide a bit of a shock, and for me an unsettling memory...

DESERT GILA

Desert flowers are not to be picked - rare gems not to be disturbed - but I'll confess that I picked one once, right by the house, by way of a presentation, an offering, in an attempt to truncate the route of a woman headed ineluctably into her next phase. It was that day when that which you had believed would last forever, is ended. A desert flower did not impress. Shared concerns, mutual respect, and unspeakable intimacies quite forsaken, she walked out the door with a look on her face that would flush a covey of quail. Tough. Tougher than me. Tougher than I would ever want to be. My desert flower along the San Francisco River was beautiful but reminiscent. I left it alone. It will be some time before I shall risk such as that again.

~ ~ ~ ~ ~ ~

It was the night when the moon would fill its form entirely. I knew it wouldn't show for a while in that steep walled canyon and I knew the fishing would be better before it did, for, according to catfish lore, big cats are more active during the dark of the moon. In the gathering dusk I was late making any supper. I wasn't hungry. I had a pole line in the water on the Frisco side. I had been unable to gather any suitable live bait, had to make do with beef liver. If I couldn't catch a big cat here I wasn't going to catch one this trip. I wasn't optimistic.

Signs of life, my pole line began to drift off *upstream*, and I set the hook. It took a good five minutes with the fish working the current to his advantage and my wrists and forearms could feel it by the time I landed the best fish of the trip so far by honest angling - a twenty inch Channel Cat. He was well tapered and slick with a fine, dark green back easing into a white belly and black speckle-spots on the sides. I rebaited the hook with an outsize chunk of liver, propped the rod into solid

202

security and commenced to clean my fish. It didn't take long and he was crisping in the fry pan. Hungry now, I was crouched in the sand with my back to the Frisco lifting filets with a fork when I looked up and saw Rojo sitting off a little ways with his head and ears cocked high and to one side in a good likeness to the old RCA Victor dog. He could hear something I couldn't. I turned around and what he was hearing was the sound of the drag letting line off the reel; the pole was bent into an alarming geometry; the fish wasn't but a few yards of taking all the monofilament away!

I grabbed the pole, hopped up on the rock ledge overlooking the San Francisco River and, tightening the drag, lay into that fish. I was hooked to the bottom but the bottom kept moving away! I jumped down, waded some shallows downstream towards the fish, then up onto this little gravel bar that split the rivers where I began to run and by all of this gained back a bunch of line. With the fish out in front of me now (he did not want to enter the rapids just below) I watched my line trail an animal's struggling route through the long, green pool, tied to the unknown monster below.

When, using light tackle, you are overmatched by a big fish you know you must keep pressure as close to the breaking point as your skill allows. You can never let the fish rest. He will never tire just swimming around; you must make him work at swimming. The longer he's out there swimming around the greater the chance he'll lose the hook, wear through the line, or wrap the line around some underwater structure. But apply too much pressure, just for an instant, and he's gone. The line breaks, or the rod breaks or the hook straightens. You protect your line and rod by keeping the rod at a sharp angle with the fish and by setting your drag to give just ahead of the breaking

DESERT GILA

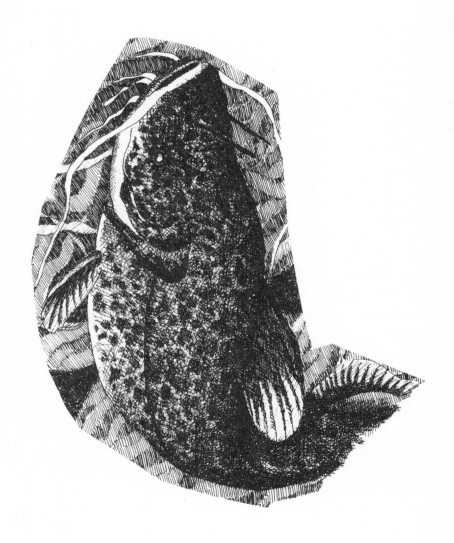

point. I knew all this, in theory and in practice, but when that fish surfaced briefly just before dark I knew there would be no landing soon. Not with a whippy spinning rod and six pound test line.

He'd been making these long almost leisurely runs (leisurely for him!), holding to the bottom between times, pumping the rod with head shakes, and I think he came up to see what he was tied to - one of those big ol' flatheads: a dark, vaguely mottled back, a body as long as your leg, a head pushing half a foot between the eyes and a mouth that could swallow a grapefruit, muskrat, or trophy trout.

After that it wasn't long. The line jumped back out of the water, landing over my shoulder, parted inches above the hook. He'd cut through the leader with his raspy teeth.

It was dark as I walked back upstream to camp. Rojo had followed me down. As we returned a tomcat sat on a rock ledge, watching intently with night eyes. I had nothing for him.

My catfish filets were overdone, and cold, but we all shared a meal. I tied on another hook and returned bait to water. For most of the night I sat along that rock ledge watching the waters; the full moon showed up, and under its peculiar light on rock and water I caught a soft-shelled snapping turtle sixteen inches across the back and another nice Channel Cat. Interesting. However, I didn't keep them. The one I'd wanted was gone.

Yet one can always find solace in a living river. It is never still, never staid; hiding its prizes, providing glimpses, it holds a continual promise of things to come. One need never fear therein the final offering. There would always be another. Surely there would be another.

~ ~ ~ ~ ~ ~

DESERT GILA

I left my camp along the San Francisco/Gila River with the sun well up later that day. I was in no position to stay a year or two. I could have stayed for several more days. I was tempted. But I knew I'd be back and the touch of it was all I wanted for now. Holding to my own cryptic promises, the crew and I shoved off. We ran maybe fifty yards down the Frisco side before joining the Gila in a pretty good shot of rapids.

The twelve mile run through the rest of the Gila/Arizona Box was the equal of anything I'd seen - a fine canyon float with the remnants of the mining days decaying along the river banks and adjacent hills, Eagle Creek coming in on the north side like a trout stream, a wonderful riparian display and a goodly number of lively rapids to give it all animation. I lined down two of these rapids; I ran the rest without incident. I was beginning to learn how to handle a canoe.

Approaching Bonita Creek the hills began to fall back away from the river, mighty Mt. Graham stood dark and forested in the distance and on the shore a pale, willowy, desert type coyote stopped drinking to stare at us. Though he remained motionless amidships, I've never seen such intensity in a tomcat. Rojo trembled and whimpered on the front seat. Our coyote didn't move till we'd passed by and when he did he simply disappeared, quick as a bird, light as a cloud. With the spring shedding of his winter coat he was pretty scruffy looking, but there's no finer mosaic than one of those pale coyotes pelted out prime in winter. Most of the ones up in Minnesota had been bigger, more wolflike animals, thick-furred and dark-coated. I remember one lovely, lithe, silver-gray animal though, who ran before Rojo's daddy and two others for many hours before they bayed him up. At ten below I followed the race on

206

snowshoes, found him backed in under a blowdown with the pack screaming triumph all around. The coyote is North America's premier game animal. There's nothing you can hunt that's faster, smarter, tougher all in one. I had mixed emotions (still do) about killing, skinning and selling the hide off that silvery Minnesota brush wolf. But I did. Seeing his counterpart along the Gila, I remembered him well, floating a desert river.

At Bonita Creek I stopped at the roadhead, seeking to hitch a ride to a telephone. But there was no one around. Down river then, and the Gila took on an ugly cast for the first time since I'd marked its waters at Bead Spring. A wide flood plain here, no trees, heavily silted water and the work of incipient construction all around. A low diversion dam was a minor obstacle. I lifted right over the top and thereafter let Rojo run the bank for a ways.

Some five miles below Bonita Creek I came to a major diversion dam populated by a bunch of cars and pickups and folks fishing, swimming, enjoying the desert water. Pulling in on the north side, a husky sort of guy in his forties with more of a southern than southwestern accent greeted me, rounded up his son and without my asking helped me get the boat over the dam and out of the river.

"Where you comin' from?"

I told him. He shook his head and smiled. "Well damn! And a cat!"

"I need to find a phone," I said..."call my ride."

"How much it cost your ride come get ya?"

"A tank of gas."

"Hell, I'll run you home for a tank of gas."

"Home's a long ways. You run me home from here I'll pay more than gas."

DESERT GILA

We loaded the boat and the hound dog and that pesky tomcat in the bed of the pickup. Then Charles Dixon of Arkansas made a short run into Safford, Arizona to quickly arrange this unplanned excursion with his good wife (she must have been).

He wanted to take the back way, the high road, up Highway 666 and on over to Mule Creek and that was fine with me. He told me that two hundred miles down the Gila River with a dog and a cat was quite something to do. I remembered how, before I'd done it, the forest ranger at the Gila Wilderness station had told me he didn't believe that river run had been traveled before, all in one. I anticipated my accomplishment then, and put the phrases beside my name - "Wilderness Expedition," "Backpacker," Whitewater King!" Having done it, I wasn't so sure. It was already beginning to seem like a piece of cake, no less meaningful for that. Most anyone could have done it, had he or she the interest and the time.

I gazed out across the desert, cholla flats, and no sign of the Gila in sight, the pickup steady and smooth at sixty-five. And it made me sleepy. And in spite of a good conversation on how to catch big catfish in the deep South and the great Southwest, I kept closing my eyes. Every time I did I was back on the river.

EPILOGUE

...Awake as we crossed the New Mexico line, across the high plains by Mule Creek, down Highway 180 towards Cliff. The blue/black Mogollón Range (the source), no longer snow-capped, stood in distant view, overbearing and pervasive. As we crossed over the low bridge the driver slowed without comment...

I looked down river at dusk to see if I could imagine a canoe, a traveler, his two friends, all in concert with the current. My imagination failed me. The Gila had changed; it really didn't look the same at all. The trip was over.

There will be other river trips of course. Each will offer its peculiar value. But as for revelations, what you can learn on a river trip is nothing you couldn't have learned long ago on a good day with your eyes wide open - that every time you round a bend you're left with something new to try and understand. An informed philosophy would call this opportunity. The opportunity remains.

Meanwhile one is left with the memories certainly, a few laments perhaps, and with luck some dear goodbyes. Lovers, rivers, pass on. One can only touch it while it's there. But handle it gently.

Portions of *Gila Descending* originally appeared in somewhat different form in *Basin & Range* and the Albuquerque *Journal*.

~ ~ ~ ~ ~ ~ ~ ~ ~ ~ ~ ~ ~ ~ ~ ~

M.H. Salmon lives in Grant County New Mexico where he spends as much time as he can fishing for catfish and hunting with his hounds.

Fred Barraza lives near Silver City, New Mexico. He is the cover artist for *Tales of the Chase* and *Home is the River*, also available from High-Lonesome Books.

HIGH-LONESOME BOOKS

"Published in the Greatest Country Out-of-Doors"

At HIGH-LONESOME BOOKS we have a great variety of titles for enthusiasts of the Southwest and the great Outdoors - new, used, and rare books of the following:

Southwest History

Wilderness Adventure

Natural History

Hunting

Sporting Dogs

Mountain Men

Fishing

Country Living

Environment

Our brochure/list is FREE for the asking. Write or call.

HIGH-LONESOME BOOKS
P. O. Box 878
Silver City, New Mexico
88062
505-388-3763

Also, come visit our new bookshop in the country at High-Lonesome Road near Silver City